ALFRED ADLER

LITERATURE AND LIFE SERIES
(Formerly Modern Literature and World Dramatists)
GENERAL EDITOR: PHILIP WINSOR

Selected list of titles:

Complete list of titles in the series available from publisher on request.

ALFRED
ADLER

Josef Rattner

Translated from the German
by Harry Zohn

FREDERICK UNGAR PUBLISHING CO.
New York

Library of Congress Cataloging in Publication Data

Rattner, Josef.
  Alfred Adler.

  Translation of: Individualpsychologie.
  Bibliography: p.
  Includes index.
  1. Psychoanalysis. 2. Self. 3. Adler, Alfred,
1870–1937. I. Title.
BF173.F364413 1983   150.19'53   82–40251
ISBN 0-8044-5988-6

Translated from the German by arrangement with the author, who holds the German copyright.

Contents

Chronology

1870	Born on February 7 in Vienna as the second son of a grain merchant. Grows up with five siblings.
1888	Graduates from secondary school and begins medical studies at the University of Vienna.
1895	Receives his medical degree and works at a Vienna hospital and an outpatient clinic.
1897	Marries Raissa Timofeyevna from Moscow.
1898	Establishes himself first as an ophthalmologist, later as a general practitioner, and finally as a psychiatrist in Vienna. In medical practice there until 1927.
1899–1900	First encounter with Freud.
1902 ff.	Participates in the Wednesday evening discussions at Freud's home.
1904	*Der Arzt als Erzieher* [The physician as educator].
1907	*Studie über die Minderwertigkeit von Organen.* [Study of organ inferiority].
1910	Becomes chairman of the Vienna group of the Psychoanalytic Association and coeditor of *Zentralblatt für Psychoanalyse*.
1911	Breaks with Freud over four lectures before members of Freud's circle entitled "Zur Kritik der Freudschen Sexualtheorie des Seelenlebens" [Critique of Freud's sexual theory of emotional life]. Founds the association for "free psychoanalysis," later named Verein für Individualpsychologie [Association for Individual Psychology].

1912   Lays the theoretical foundation for individ-
            ual psychology in his work *Über den ner-
            vösen Charakter* [The neurotic constitu-
            tion].

1913   *Heilen und Bilden* [Healing and educating]
            (with Carl Furtmüller).

1914   Founds the *Internationale Zeitschrift für
            Individualpsychologie* (IZI) [International
            Journal for Individual Psychology].

1914–16   Army doctor in Cracow, Brno, and Vienna.

1920   Teaches at the Pädagogium of the City of
            Vienna and by 1934 establishes about thirty
            child guidance clinics in Vienna. *Praxis und
            Theorie der Individualpsychologie* [Practice
            and theory of individual psychology].

1923 ff.   Extensive lecture tours through Germany,
            Denmark, Holland, England, etc.

1924   Appointed Lecturer at the Pädagogium.

1926   First lecture trip to the United States.

1927   *Menschenkenntnis* [Understanding human
            nature].

1928   *Technik der Individualpsychologie. Teil 1:
            Die Kunst, eine Lebens- und Krankheitsge-
            schichte zu lesen.* [Technique of individual
            psychology. Part 1. The art of interpreting a
            life and case history].

1929 ff.   Extended sojourns in the United States, al-
            though his family stays in Vienna. Accepts a
            lectureship at Columbia University and
            opens a practice as a psychotherapist in New
            York City.

1929   *Individualpsychologie in der Schule* [Indi-
            vidual psychology in the school].

1930   *Technik der Individualpsychologie. Teil 2:
            Die Seele des schwererziehbaren Kindes.*
            [The psyche of the difficult child]. *The Edu-
            cation of Children. Das Problem der Homo-
            sexualität* [The problem of homosexuality].

1931   *What Life Should Mean to You.*

1932   *Der Sinn des Lebens* [The meaning of life].

1932 ff.   Visiting Professor of Medical Psychology at
            Long Island College, New York.

1933   *Religion und Individualpsychologie* [Reli-
            gion and individual psychology] (with Ernst
            Jahn).

1934   Leaves his home in Austria and moves to
            New York permanently with his family.

1935   Founds the *International Journal of Indi-
            vidual Psychology.*

1937   Dies on May 28 in Aberdeen, Scotland,
            while on a lecture tour.

Preface

In the psychological discussions of the present, Alfred Adler's *individual psychology* is increasingly appreciated. As one of the great classical systems of depth psychology, it has made important contributions to the understanding of human nature and promoted both the theory and the practice of depth psychology. Adler's structure of ideas, the originality and future potential of which have not been exhausted to this day, continues to be a force in the works of almost all recent writers on related subjects; in particular, it has prepared the ground for very significant changes in the fields of education and guidance. These changes, to be sure, have not matched the hopes of this great and kindly humanitarian, and they reflect only weakly the results expected from consistent application of his doctrines to the communal life of individuals and nations. Adler lived long enough to witness, shortly before his death, the resurgence in politics of the mad fictions of the will to power, fictions that brought about World War II.

In the frenzy of that war Adler's humane teachings were barely heeded, and consequently they do not at present enjoy the dissemination they deserve. This is probably also due to the chaotic situation of our civilization following the worst and bloodiest war in a "cultural" history rife with brutality. A world that emerged from global military entanglements only to regress immediately to the darkness and disillusionment of a prolonged cold war is not a fertile soil for a doctrine that stresses the universal fellowship of all human beings. An age in which atomic rearmament conjures up the horrors of the total destruction of mankind and in which for the sake of ideological differences a deaf ear is turned to the admonitions of the human conscience offers a rough path for Adler's view of life, a view that is imbued with the spirit of peace and nonviolence.

But Adler will go down in history as more than a humanist. His pioneering achievement was in the field of psychology, and he enriched this field with innovations of inestimable value. It is to his lasting credit that he was the first to demonstrate the artificiality of psychoanalytic theory and its remoteness from life. His critique rocked the Freudian structure—the one-sided sexual theory, the fanciful Oedipus complex—to its foundations for the first time. Adler replaced these concepts, which are based on natural science and the ideal of a biochemical and causal psychology, with an understanding psychology which is appropriate to man as a social and value-oriented creature. His *Menschenkenntnis* ("understanding of human nature") completely eschewed the energetic metaphors which, under the guise of science, make living things take on the rigid form and frigidity of ice flowers, but instead became a pliant tool whose efficacy could repeatedly be tested and demonstrated in terms of the uniqueness and distinctiveness of the individual.

Many concepts created by Adler have become part of everyday language: *inferiority complex* (Minderwertigkeitskomplex), *social interest* (Gemeinschaftsgefühl), *striving for superiority* (Geltungsstreben). Even experts using these terms are fond of forgetting who discovered and opened these gates to emotional life. Those who particularly do not like to mention Adler's name are the authors who are giving his insights new life in their own theories under other names, and sometimes giving them outstanding literary and scientific styling. Anyone familiar with the development of depth psychology who traces the ideas found in contemporary authors to their origins will become increasingly aware of how comprehensive the aftereffects of Adler's creativity are among his friends—and his opponents. The great humanitarian himself would probably only have smiled at this and settled for the satisfaction of knowing that even though his name may not be spread everywhere, his work is.

The present book attempts to present an introduction to individual psychology. The author belongs to the Adlerian school, and his psychotherapeutic practice is based upon individual psychology. In his high regard for Alfred Adler's work and personality he would like to draw the attention of laymen and fellow professionals alike to the ideas of individual psychology, which contain the most valuable seeds for the further development of depth psychology. The fact that Adler's teachings are also available in the paraphrases of neopsychoanalysis does not seem adequate to the author. Water, too, is purer at its source than in the lowlands of the broad streams.

The ideas contained in this book were first published in German in 1961. They are thus an early work of the author, who has since learned some additional things. Hence almost everything has been fundamentally reworked, revised, and expanded in order to reflect the present state of scholarship. It is very gratifying that an English translation of this work can now appear in the United States. May it promote and solidify interest there in Alfred Adler and in individual psychology!

Josef Rattner

Striving for personal power is a deleterious delusion and poisons the communal life of human beings. Anyone who desires human community must renounce the striving for power over others. Using force to attain success seems like a natural idea to many. Let us admit it: it *seems* to be the simplest way to gain by means of force everything that is good and promises happiness, or even that which is part of an inevitable development. Where in human life or human history has such a plan succeeded? Wherever we look, the employment of even mild force arouses a counterwill, even where it is clear that the good of the person being subdued is intended. The patriarchal system and enlightened absolutism are frightening vestiges of this kind. No people has endured even its god without opposition. Take a person or a people into someone else's sphere of power, and immediately resistance will stir, overtly or covertly, and it will not disappear until all fetters are shaken off.

Alfred Adler, "Psychologie der Macht" [Psychology of Power], in *Gewalt und Gewaltlosigkeit* [Violence and Nonviolence], Zurich, 1928.

1

Alfred Adler: Humanistic Psychologist

When Alfred Adler died in 1937 in Aberdeen, Scotland, of acute heart failure, he was 67 years old and at the height of his fame. Lecture tours took him to many cities of the Old and the New World, where he found ready listeners and pupils for his *individual psychology*. Everywhere there were local groups dedicated to the dissemination of this so-called understanding depth psychology, and everywhere Adler won physicians, educators, social workers, psychologists, and psychotherapists as friends and supporters. The charm and kindliness of his personality enabled him to build bridges effortlessly to all men of goodwill who wished to work for the improvement of human and social conditions. Adler did not just teach, he also *lived* his message of *Gemeinschaftsgefühl* (social interest), i.e., solidarity and mutual aid in all areas of human communal living. Thus he found open ears for his new science of healthy and pathological emotional life as well as for his *ethics of personality*, which profoundly influenced the study of human nature.

Who was Alfred Adler, and how did the theory and practice of his depth psychology develop? How did he become the cultural leader that we respect and admire?

Adler was born in 1870 near Vienna, the son of

a Jewish businessman. It gave him pleasure to relate that he had had a real "Viennese street urchin childhood." He spent much time with friends and schoolmates, and this may have given him an early understanding of human nature. In his father, to whom he had emotionally attached himself to a greater degree than to his mother, he had a good model for industriousness, sense of duty, and social-mindedness. The father seems to have been particularly fond of this son too, because at an early age he took him along on extensive walks and instructed him in his practical wisdom.

Adler was at first a mediocre pupil but later had a great deal of success, and this encouraged further learning efforts on his part. After completing his secondary education he enrolled at the University of Vienna as a medical student. Unfortunately we have hardly any documents from Adler's student days, and there is little about them in his autobiographical writings. What courses did he take in addition to his prescribed medical studies? What books were read by the man who all his life was an avid reader? It is very regrettable that we know so little about Adler's student years, for often the story of a great man's youth is exceedingly illuminating for the later structuring of his life work. If one knows the beginnings of such a man's ideas, one understands much better why they were bound to develop in this way or that. Invariably even the most subtle intellectual creations are based on personal experiences. In the case of Adler we have only intimations of what he experienced, thought, hoped, and strove for as a young man. The origins of his brilliant psychology are largely obscure.

At any rate, in those years he appears to have been close to the socialist movement. That was nothing unusual for a young Jewish intellectual.

Many leading theoreticians of Austro-Marxism were highly educated Jews. Adler, however, seems to have had reservations about Social Democracy and bolshevism at an early age. We may presume that he was inspired, among other things, by the libertarian and antiauthoritarian socialism of Kropotkin and Bakunin. In Adler's writings there is no reference to Prince Peter Kropotkin's *Gegenseitige Hilfe in der Natur und Menschenwelt* [Mutual aid in nature and the human world], a work then much discussed, but since Adler's psychology is conceived in the spirit of this high-minded social philosopher, there must have been some points of contact.

Adler's first literary work was *Gesundheitsbüchlein für das Schneidergewerbe* [Health handbook for the tailoring trade], an early documentation of his sense of social responsibility, published in 1897. By that time he already was a physician active in many branches of medicine. Around 1902 there took place his epoch-making encounter with Sigmund Freud. Adler became a member of the so-called *Mittwochsgesellschaft* [Wednesday Society], which met every week in Freud's apartment at No. 19 Berggasse. A dozen adherents of the new psychoanalytic movement, mostly physicians, met there regularly to discuss the fundamentals of the new doctrine. From the *Protokolle der Wiener Psychoanalytischen Vereinigung* [Minutes of the Vienna Psychoanalytic Society] we learn that Adler was one of the most zealous members of this discussion group, which dealt with psychotherapy and depth psychology in all their applications. While reading these minutes one is struck by the fact that Adler was one of the most cultivated, most benevolent, and most humane participants in that group. He also seems to have enjoyed Freud's high esteem to an exceptional degree. At some time or other

Freud is said to have told a visitor who accused him of favoritism in the case of Adler, "But he is the only personality in this circle!" Adler must surely have been outstanding when compared with Wilhelm Stekel, Otto Rank, Eduard Hitschmann, Fritz Wittels, Isidor Sadger, and others.

In later years Adler objected to being called a pupil of Freud. He regarded himself as a collaborator in Freud's circle, about which he had reservations at an early date. Adler was grateful for the chance to work with the creator of psychoanalysis, but he also struck out on his own paths, considering his own thought as independent.

In 1907 Adler published his *Studie über die Minderwertigkeit von Organen* [Study of organ inferiority]. This early study already displays his originality. Adler bases himself on Darwin's and Lamarck's doctrines about the natural evolution of living creatures. For him every living thing is in evolution. But what does an organism do if in the struggle for existence it is equipped with so-called inferior organs? Here Adler postulates the law of compensation and overcompensation. An organism has a chance to make up for organic defects; the weaknesses of certain organs are compensated for by other organs. The most important site of compensation, however, is the emotional life. With the aid of his emotional function a person can transform biological defects into strengths. The psyche is an organ of foresight, of "attentiveness to life" and the establishment of social relations. Where communal ties prevail, a person transcends his biological limitations. Civilization is the site of all useful compensations and overcompensations. But where a person's social interest remains underdeveloped, biological and social handicaps evoke unsuitable responses, leading to character anomalies, neuroses,

psychoses, criminality, and what we now call psychosomatic disturbances. With the above-mentioned study, incidentally, Adler laid the foundation
for psychosomatic medicine, a field that has as-
sumed great importance today.

Adler also demonstrated in further essays and
treatises that he was far from an uncritical acceptance of the dogmas of psychoanalytic theory. Thus
at an early age he doubted the universal validity of
the *Oedipus complex* and the necessity of the *libido
theory*, criticizing the latter for its unquestionable
physicalism and mechanistic interpretation of the
psyche. The *pansexualism* of psychoanalysis appeared more than dubious to him. Inspired by
Nietzsche and other authors, he was skeptical about
the opinion that a person seeks pleasure and nothing
but pleasure in all activities. Thus he could not
bring himself to see in every dream a *wish dream*
that merely points back to the dreamer's childhood.
For him everything emotional was also oriented toward the future. A person wants to grow and develop; he activates his emotional life in order to
come to terms with his environment and in order to
divine and shape the future. Thus the human psyche must be interpreted teleologically. Freud's
causal constructs and energy concepts derive from
the materialistic natural science of the nineteenth
century from which Adler disassociated himself as
a matter of principle. Thus he increasingly came
into conflict with Sigmund Freud, making a break
between the two great pioneers of depth psychology
inevitable.

Their dispute reached its climax in 1910 and
1911. At the Psychoanalytic Congress in Weimar
(1910) Freud had his favorite pupil, Sandor Fer-
enczi, propose that in future all treatises on psychoanalysis be reviewed by C. G. Jung, who had

meanwhile become president of the International Association and was regarded by Freud as the "crown prince." Adler rightly regarded this as an abridgment of intellectual freedom and lodged a vehement protest. Compromises were found, but the rift had already manifested itself clearly.

In 1911 Adler gave four lectures before the Wednesday Society under the title *"Zur Kritik der Freudschen Sexualtheorie des Seelenlebens"* [A critique of Freud's sexual theory of emotional life]. Since these lectures cast doubt upon almost all fundamental positions of psychoanalysis, it was logical that he should have been asked more or less directly to leave the Psychoanalytic Society. According to Adler, infantile sexuality did not play a decisive, neurosis-causing role; the Oedipus complex only illuminated the contest between a child's self-assertion and parental authority (in a misleading sexual analogy); and *repression* was dependent on the ambition and vanity of the neurotic:

My findings show that concealed behind everything that one can designate as sexual there are far more significant connections—namely, the masculine protest concealed behind sexuality. By way of refuting the objection that masculine protest and repression are one and the same thing I have attempted to prove today that repression is only a partial effect of the masculine protest. . . . One can no longer speak of a complex of libidinous desires and fantasies; we must view the Oedipus complex as a partial phenomenon of a larger psychic dynamism, as a phase of masculine protest, and this will facilitate a deeper understanding of the nature of neurosis.

Adler left Freud's circle and took more than a dozen of his adherents with him. These seem to have been largely socialists, and among them was Carl Furtmüller, later a well-known politician in the Austrian Social Democratic Party. Adler now founded his *Verein für freie Psychoanalyse* [Society for Free Psychoanalytic Research]. Soon, however, he called his doctrine *individual psychology*, indicating that the exploration of the individual personality was at the center of his interest. Nevertheless, his doctrine always was *social psychology* as well, for no branch of depth psychology placed as much emphasis on the social interrelationship of all human beings as did Adler's theory. In this respect it differs in an especially gratifying way from psychoanalysis, which views man as an "asocial, lustful, aggressive beast."

As early as 1912 Adler published his major work, *Über den nervösen Charakter: Grundzüge einer vergleichenden Individual-Psychologie und Psychotherapie* (published in English as *The Neurotic Constitution*). This work made it readily apparent that Adler's doctrine was not simply a polemical variant of Freud's findings but an original, independent, and comprehensive outline which combined normal psychology and psychopathology in one scheme. In the wealth of its viewpoints and the breadth of its vision this magnificent book is certainly comparable to Freud's *Traumdeutung* [*The Interpretation of Dreams*] of 1900. It introduces as basic components of emotional life the well-known concepts of *feeling of inferiority* (Minderwertigkeitsgefühl), *striving for superiority* (Geltungsstreben), and *social interest* (Gemeinschaftsgefühl). Proceeding from the unity of healthy and pathological emotional life, Adler views neurosis as merely an accentuation of human helplessness and existential problems. Neurotics and psychotics are not basically different from so-called normal people. They are victims of an education and a civilization that are alien to life, cause illness, discourage all of us, and keep us from making a contribution to soci-

ety. Thus we become entangled in phantoms and
fictions. As disheartened human beings we do not
believe ourselves to be capable of solving the social
tasks of life—work, love, and community— in a
fruitful manner. The withdrawal from reality into
the shelter of pampering and self-indulgence is now
termed *neurosis*; it is an artificial product of a false
and unsuitable education. Such a neurosis can be
cured by improving the patient's self-esteem,
which, to be sure, is possible only if his feelings are
channeled in a humanitarian direction. To Adler,
psychotherapy was reeducation, with the therapist
having to take charge of the socialization that had
been neglected in childhood by the mother and the
father. While Freud faced his patients as a cool and
detached observer, Adler was more of a humorous
and amiable counselor and helper. He did not regard his patients as research objects, as expressed
in Freud's "couch therapy." For Adler a person who
consulted him was always a "partner in conversation," and the psychotherapeutic treatment appeared as a conversation between two fellow human
beings of equal worth and with equal rights. Many
theoretical and practical innovations were introduced into depth psychology and psychotherapy by
Adler. Thus it is ridiculous for some psychoanalysts
to assert, as did Freud, that only Adler's "ambition"
caused him to break away from Freud. It is well
known that one year later C. G. Jung also turned
away from orthodox psychoanalysis. Was this ambition as well? In science, at any rate, it is very useful if the pupils of a master are ambitious in this
way, for only a multiplicity and variety of viewpoints can further scientific research. Single-mind-
edness may be desirable for a political or religious
faith, but in science it means the death of reason.

Heilen und Bilden [Healing and educating], a collection of essays edited by Adler and Furtmüller in 1913, supplied early evidence of the great interest of individual psychology in problems of education in the parental home and in school. Freud at first showed little interest in education; only at a much later date did psychoanalysis gain access to pedagogical problems. Adler, however, was fascinated by educational questions from the beginning. In education he saw the greatest chance for prevention of neuroses, psychoses, and criminality. Hence he never tired of pointing out the necessity of giving all parents and teachers psychological training. The very fact that Adler formulated his teachings with a certain simplicity of language indicates his desire to make psychology accessible to everyone. Individual psychology was to become a comprehensive body of knowledge of human nature. It was to enable every thinking person to understand himself and his fellow human beings. Adler believed that an increased understanding of interpersonal relationships would bring about a more sensible form of individual and collective living. Even in those years Adler championed the antiauthoritarian, nonviolent education which, almost always misunderstood, has today become a catchword. He speaks of an education through love, reason, and consistency of language. If one reads *Heilen und Bilden* almost 70 years after its publication, one is surprised at how much of what is demanded there still awaits realization. Mankind is quick in its technical progress but slow in its educational and cultural development.

The outbreak of World War I in 1914 meant a great shock for Alfred Adler. He did not allow himself to be swept away by the wave of nationalistic and militaristic megalomania. Here he saw the "striving for power" which he had diagnosed as being at work in unadulterated mass psychology. The leaders of nations craftily misused the social interest of the masses for their obscure purposes. Thus, more than ten million people died for a collective delusion. Adler, who spent the war as an army doctor in Cracow and Vienna, realized more clearly than ever the importance of a mental hygiene encompassing all mankind.

In 1918, in starving and chaotic Vienna, the rebuilding of the individual psychology movement was tackled with renewed energy. Before the war Adler had founded his *Internationale Zeitschrift für Individualpsychologie* [International Journal of Individual Psychology]. This publication had been discontinued in wartime but was now revived. Adler's pupils again gathered around their teacher and started to examine how they could make themselves useful in providing information and therapy.

The city of Vienna, which had a Social Democratic administration, was very favorably disposed toward the teachings of individual psychology, for they could be interpreted as a psychology in the spirit of socialist humanism. Thus Adler received valuable support from government offices when in 1920 he established educational guidance centers, in which parents and children received counseling and treatment free of charge. Adler himself carried on educational guidance in the presence of numerous doctors and educators, who by listening received an introduction to the problems of childrearing. These guidance centers in socialist Vienna were the origin of the child guidance movement, which later spread to all civilized countries.

Although Adler's coworkers included a number of Social Democrats and communists, he never com-

mitted himself to the ideology of any political party.
Adler wished to remain an independent humanist.
Shortly after World War I he made an analysis of
the Russian Revolution and came to the conclusion
that the Bolsheviks had embraced the spirit of domination and suppression. His psychological knowledge of human nature led him to predict that the
Bolshevik regime would soon degenerate and once
more result in tyranny, since power and violence
attract pathological types, who rise to the top in authoritarian circumstances and are able to act out
their mental illnesses recklessly. The dictatorship
of Stalin confirmed this bleak prognosis in horrible
fashion. The psychology of our era's dictators is
composed of numerous illustrations and documen-
tations of Adler's theses on the inferiority complex
and the striving to be godlike. Adler did not fall prey
to the admiration of bolshevism displayed by many
intellectuals. With great discernment he recognized that here again, as in the war, the social interest of the people was being put to work for the
power interests of a small pseudoelite.

Around 1920 Adler's life work seemed to be approaching a period of great development and flow-
ering. In those years he published his second major
work, *Praxis und Theorie der Individualpsychologie* [*The Practice and Theory of Individual Psychology*]. To be sure, the School of Medicine of the
University of Vienna had rejected Adler's *Über den
nervösen Charakter* [*The Neurotic Constitution*] as
a *Habilitationsarbeit* (a dissertation required to
qualify for a university appointment). A committee
of narrow-minded professors of medicine under the
chairmanship of the famous psychiatrist Julius Wag-
ner von Jauregg certified that the brilliant psychologist and psychotherapist was not qualified to teach
medical students. Adler bitterly recorded this re-

jection in his preface to the second edition of *Über den nervösen Charakter*, though he clearly realized that the committee's decision constituted no genuine value judgment on his thought.

The city of Vienna then appointed him to train teachers at the *Pädagogium* [Pedagogical Institute], and thus Adler was able to work actively toward the improvement of educational methods, which was such a central concern of his. He had great success in arousing the enthusiasm of young and old teachers alike for antiauthoritarian, sympathetic education and training of young people. Two experienced educators, Oskar Spiel and Ferdinand Birnbaum, supported him in these endeavors. Under the aegis of Adler these educators later created the *Individualpsychologische Versuchsschule Wien* [Vienna Experimental School of Individual Psychology], which became world-renowned as an educational experiment.

Many patients came to Adler from all over the world in order to get psychotherapeutic treatment from him. He also undertook numerous lecture tours throughout Europe, and thus within a short time local groups devoted to individual psychology were founded in dozens of cities. Adler was a magnificent speaker, who was able to win people over to his ideals. His lectures were devoid of theatrics and rhetorical devices. But it was precisely his unadorned and easily comprehensible speaking style, which eliminated the ballast of erudition, that inspired all listeners imbued with social interest. Thus Adler was able to recruit thousands of adherents for his doctrine; among these, people in the service professions predominated.

The political climate in Austria became increasingly unstable, however, and it was none too favorable for the further dissemination of individual psychology. Soon after the war the middle-class center, in which the Catholic church was very powerful, reconstituted itself. Conservative and reactionary circles looked askance at the power of the workers' parties, which was restraining the machinations of capitalism and Catholicism. Mussolini had already shown in Italy how one could smash Marxism and reduce the Social Democrats and the labor unions to impotence. This appeared exemplary to the Austrian fascists, and they single-mindedly built an army prepared for civil war, the so-called *Heimwehr* [Home Defense] under the leadership of Prince Starhemberg. They were waiting for an opportunity to finish off socialism in all its varieties.

Engelbert Dollfuss, who had become federal chancellor of Austria in 1932, abolished the constitution by means of a coup d'état and governed without a parliament, supported by the *Vaterländische Front* [Patriotic Front] as the sole political party. Thus he wished to create an Austrian *Ständestaat* [corporative state] under the patronage of Italian fascism. In 1934 the suppressed Social Democrats staged a belated and poorly organized uprising; this was bloodily put down and ended with the total subjugation of the people by the clerical-fascist regime. Dollfuss, to be sure, was not destined to enjoy his victory over the leftist parties; in 1934 he was assassinated during a National Socialist *Putsch*.

An Austria that was overshadowed in the south by Mussolini and from 1933 on in the north by Hitler was not a good place for Adler to propagate his doctrine of reason, freedom, and solidarity. As early as the late twenties Catholicism had wiped out many achievements of educational reform, reinstating corporal punishment and morning prayers in the schools. Socialists were sent to prison or to concentration camps. The spirit of the fascist epoch ex-

pressed itself in the Alpine republic as well, and
Austria became an inhospitable country for individual psychology. Added to this was the fact that many
depth psychologists were of Jewish descent. Austrian anti-Semitism, which had in his Vienna years
inspired Hitler to adopt his obscure *Weltanschauung*, placed many obstacles in the path of Jewish citizens. Adler searched for opportunities to shift
the focal point of his activity away from Austria, and
he came to consider the English-speaking countries
to an increased extent.

As early as 1926 he had given lectures in the
United States and had been astonished at the open-
mindedness and genuine interest with which he
and his teachings had been received there. Number
3 of the *Internationale Zeitschrift für Individualpsychologie* contains the following report about a
lecture given by Adler in 1927 upon his return from
his first trip to America:

Adler's lecture took place in the auditorium of the His-
tological Institute of the University of Vienna. There he
was received with joyous affection and enthusiasm by an
audience of hundreds and warmly greeted by the chair-
man of the evening, Prof. D. E. Oppenheim. Adler's first
lecture about his American trip was devoted to the enormous interest which the entire population of North America has in education. This interest in educational questions, which is promoted by the entire American press and
supported by almost unlimited funds, was one of the main
reasons why Alfred Adler's lecture tour became a veri-
table triumphal procession of individual psychology on
American soil. During the approximately four and one-
half months of his stay in America, Adler presented the
teachings of individual psychology in more than 300 lectures and courses in the largest cities, addressing schol-
arly audiences as well as private gatherings in English.
His appearance, his doctrine, and its prime importance

for modern education met with the greatest appreciation everywhere.

One can imagine that this kind of reception and the subsequent offers of positions did not fail to make an impression on Adler. Though he had established a beautiful home on the outskirts of Vienna, he increasingly accustomed himself to the idea of emigrating. After 1926 he repeatedly traveled to the United States, finally receiving a visiting professorship in New York and in 1932 a professorship of medical psychology at Long Island College of Medicine. At that time he made a definite decision to settle in North America and give up his Austrian residence, for Europe was in increasing measure being drawn into the vortex of fascism, which in both theory and practice was the absolute counterworld to Adlerian individual psychology. There it was no longer a question of reason, mutual aid, humanitarianism, peace, and understanding among peoples. In those mass psychoses the demon of power madness held sway quite openly. People again spoke of rearmament, war, domination, violence, and murder. Adler was forced to realize that he would not be able to do much for his science of man on the European continent.

Nevertheless, he went to Europe almost every year to give lectures and training courses in the democratically governed countries. Untiringly he entered the race against the barbaric forces of his time, for he wanted to enlist as many people as possible in the cause of consideration for one's fellowman, an idea that appeared to him as the guiding star of every sensible and productive life.

It was in this spirit that he addressed lay persons and scholars, with a perfect command of both

speaking styles. Adler, the great scientist and philosopher of life, was capable of delivering lectures
on the highest level, in which scholarship and the
art of presentation were combined in a splendid
synthesis. But the same scholar and humanitarian
was able to speak, for example, at the *Volksheim
Ottakring* [community center of a Vienna workingmen's district] and present to hundreds of workers
the theory set forth in his book *Menschenkenntnis*
[1927; *Understanding Human Nature*] in such a
way that everyone understood him. Manès Sperber,
one of his pupils from those days, called Adler in a
booklet "the social genius of our time." People did
indeed flock to Adler because he did not impart to
them merely dry scholarship but humanitarianism
and human dignity. He interpreted neuroses,
anomalies of character, and human weaknesses in
such a kindly and understanding fashion that all
who listened to him felt within themselves the impulse to become better and more sensible human
beings.

Adler not only gave lectures; he also wrote a
whole series of books intended to publicize his
teachings. We shall mention here only the most important texts that he published from the end of the
twenties on. Among his very significant works are
Der Sinn des Lebens [1933; *Social Interest: A Challenge to Mankind*], and *Religion und Individualpsychologie*, 1933, Among Adler's books published
in English are *The Science of Living* (1932), *What
Life Should Mean to You* (1933), and *The Education
of Children* (1935). In all these books Adler further
developed his theory and adduced new points of
view. The depth psychologist increasingly evolved
into a philosopher, who expanded his field of vision
to the world as a whole, to the life and activities of
mankind.

Adler's book *Social Interest: A Challenge to Mankind* reads in places like a covert and overt debate with fascism. Adler was profoundly shocked at the fact that in the twentieth century such a petty, mindless, and antihumane ideology found adherents among the masses. In conversations with friends he used to shake his head and say: "In Shakespeare's play *A Midsummer Night's Dream* a man is changed into an ass, and everyone is surprised. But now—a whole people of 65 million!" By the 65 million he meant the number of *deutsche Volksgenossen* [fellow Germans, as defined by the Nazis].

The true meaning of life, according to Adler, is not power and dominion but "making a contribution to the community." Only he who serves the evolving civilization of mankind can remain mentally healthy and achieve happiness. Mental health means to develop oneself and at the same time help the community. This can be done only by rejecting authoritarianism, the cancer of our culture. Adler demonstrates the deleterious consequences of power madness in the life of neurotics, in religion, in politics, and in the economy. In a soft and yet insistent voice he recommends the ideal of humaneness, the validity of which cannot be curtailed by dictatorial "May flies":

The weal of the community and the further development of mankind are based on the eternal and imperishable demands of our ancestors. Their spirit will live forever. It is immortal, the way others are in their children. The continued existence of the human race is founded on both. . . . The question of the right way seems to me to be solved, even though we often grope in the dark. We do not wish to make a decision, but there is one thing we can say: we can consider a movement by an individual . . . and a mass movement as valuable only if they create values for eternity, for the higher development of all of mankind. Let no one refer to his own stupidity or the stupidity of others to refute this. It goes without saying that it is not a matter of possessing truth but of striving for it.

With this criterion one can try to learn from the evolution of living things and from the history of mankind what one ought to use as a guide:

This fact becomes even more convincing and perhaps even more self-evident when we ask what happened to those people who contributed nothing to the common good. The answer is that they have completely vanished. Not a trace of them has remained; they have become phys- ically and spiritually extinct. The earth has swallowed them up. Their fate was that of extinct species of animals which were unable to live in harmony with the cosmic realities. Actually, a secret law is at work here. It is as if the questioning cosmos commanded: Away with you! You have not grasped the meaning of life. You cannot extend into the future.

Even though Adler was a decided agnostic, he strikes a conciliatory note in *Religion und Indivi- dualpsychologie*, a work he coauthored with Rev- erend Ernst Jahn. Adler is prepared to concede that the idea of social interest is at work in religious faiths as well. It is not scientifically formulated, however, but uses the mythical imagery that usually does not suffice modern man. Adler did not believe in God or in the Bible, but he was inclined to col- laborate with well-disposed clergymen; he believed that if a clergyman had training in individual psy- chology, he could accomplish particularly important things for mental hygiene. In those years there ac- tually were a considerable number of clergymen in the international individual psychology movement.

It is tempting to ask what transformations Ad- ler's doctrine underwent in the twenties and thirties. Transplantation to another continent and other social and economic conditions usually has a significant influence on the intellectual shaping of a person and his thought. In point of fact, it may be noticed that from 1930 on Adler's writings occasionally displayed a different emphasis. Certain changes began to make themselves felt, though these may have been due not only to Adler's move to the United States but also to the aging process, to his greater inner mellowness. As we have already indicated, the old Adler became a "philosopher of life." As a successor of Bergson, Nietzsche, Dilthey, Kant, and many others, he was searching for the "idea of mankind" for which a person ought to live and strive. He became the *ethical teacher* for his contemporaries and for the future.

In the United States Adler encountered the philosophical doctrine of pragmatism as developed by William James, John Dewey, Charles S. Peirce, F. C. S. Schiller, and others. The pragmatists assert that we cannot find absolute truth; we should not even look for it, since this is always a waste of time. Truth is merely a name for reflections that get us ahead practically; their value for the conduct of our life determines whether we call something true. This refreshing lightheartedness in philosophizing seems to have impressed Adler in his last decades. He knew similar thought from his study of Hans Vaihinger's book *Die Philosophie des Als Ob* [*The Philosophy of As If*, 1913], which he always praised as a philosophical masterpiece. Now he encountered among American thinkers a similar skeptical attitude, which matched his own. Like the pragmatists, in his final years he emphasized common sense, preached an *evolutionary humanism* in Darwin's sense and that of his continuators, and also embraced the *Weltanschauung* of the South African

general and philosopher J. C. Smuts, who in 1930
had published a book on holism (i.e., philosophy of
totality). This was bound to appeal to Adler, since
he had himself based his entire psychology on the
observation of connections in emotional life. In contrast to the mechanistic-scientific psychology of the
nineteenth century (of which psychoanalysis still
forms part), Adler espoused the thesis that the psyche is *gestalt, structure,* and *totality.* Though he
never mentioned Wilhelm Dilthey, he also seems
to have been inspired by the latter's *hermeneutic
psychology.* But the idea postulated by Smuts that
the entire world and the cosmos should be regarded
as a totality seems to have fascinated the older
Adler. Adler's striving in his late years to enlist all
"men of good will" in a "rescue of civilization" also
strikes one as "American." Freud, too, was an educator and a humanist, but it would hardly have oc-
curred to him to go everywhere as a preacher in
order to give the widest possible dissemination to
his teachings. Considering this dissemination to
mass audiences, perhaps Adler gave too little training to his pupils, who had gathered around him in
considerable numbers. He traveled too much to de-
vote himself intensively to the character training
and theoretical instruction of his adherents. Thus
these followers constituted a rather motley crew,
something that was surely true of the Freudians as
well. Many of them were well-meaning people, but
not all who meant well had enough knowledge and
the required qualities of character. Thus Adler's
heirs, who later continued his work in his name, did
not always remain on the high level of his ethics
and his insights. But presumably that is the lot of
all great men, who are largely misunderstood by
their successors and followers.

Nevertheless, Adler's achievement in the thirties commands considerable respect. He traveled a great deal, taught wherever he found listeners, wrote his books, and treated hundreds of people in need of his counsel and his help. Phyllis Bottome, the author of a very insightful biography of Adler (*Alfred Adler: Apostle of Freedom*, 1939) tells with how much patience and humor he interested himself in everyone who sought his counsel. Most patients ended their therapy by becoming Adler's friends and fellow fighters. They joined him in order to be able to impart the insights of depth psychology to other people as well. Adler did not simply preach consideration for one's fellowmen—he *lived* it.

Phyllis Bottome has also sketched with literary skill a portrait of Adler in the circle of his pupils. After a hard day's work he would meet his friends in a café, one of his favorite places. There he was capable of spending hours of discussion with his like-minded friends about psychology, cultural questions, education, politics, and social problems. Sparkling conversation was his vital element. The small, rotund man with the warm, gleaming eyes stimulated everyone to think along with him and to think independent thoughts. With scintillating formulations he would illuminate the most difficult questions that can be raised in science and in everyday life. Many of his contemporaries have reported that he was stimulating, cheering, and encouraging to be around. A joke by Adler often lifted depressions that other psychiatrists had toyed with for months or years. The great scholar and humanitarian of world renown was apt to turn instantly into the witty street urchin he had been decades before, when he used to scuffle with other street urchins in the suburbs of Vienna. Adler never emphasized his

authority, though he had no difficulty inspiring respect. He acted as an equal among equals, but he
radiated so much dignity and humaneness that people were ready to give him credit. Even the most
mistrustful and misanthropic neurotics believed
him when he showed them the opportunities in
their seemingly failed lives. He gave them the courage to make something of themselves. The charisma
of his personality helped many people to regain
their health even before their destinies, their life
histories, and their childhood traumas had been
analyzed.

That is what Alfred Adler, the Viennese, the
citizen of the world, the psychiatrist, and the socialist humanist was like. If one looks back upon his
rich life in the service of humanity, a life that came
to an untimely end in 1937 in the Scottish city of
Aberdeen (what would Adler have been able to
achieve if fate had granted him Freud's life span of
83 years or Jung's of 86?), one can only pay tribute
to him with the beautiful words of Shakespeare's
Hamlet:

> He was a man, take him for all in all,
> We shall not look upon his like again.

2

The Theoretical Foundations of Individual Psychology

Adler's Image of Man

Adler's revolutionary transcendence of psycho-analysis is not merely an expression of new empirical findings; it originated as a different image of man and human nature. Many intellectual currents of the times flowed into individual psychology and found a new formulation in it. Freud's psychology is still entirely rooted in the mechanistic-biological nineteenth century; in it man appears as a creature of weak intelligence who is at the mercy of his all-powerful drives and instincts. His emotional life blindly obeys the unshakable compulsion of deterministic drives, which it seems illusory to revolt against. Freedom and self-determination are merely self-deceptions of the ego, which Freud, following Schopenhauer, describes as a cripple who lets a hulking blind man carry him around on his shoulders. With a certain logicality Freud's philosophy of civilization ultimately leads to a pessimism that proclaims death as the goal of all life, which means that cultural pessimism virtually degenerates into a cosmic pessimism.

Adler's progressive and social-minded view of life contrasts with Freud's basically conservative cast of thought, which in its use of "drives" jargon revived the age-old preconception of the wicked-

ness of human nature. Adler's teachings are profoundly inspired by democratic ideals. Humanistic
socialism is not only the crown of his conceptions
but their actual point of departure. This explains
why individual psychology, more than any other
branch of psychology, always describes man as a
social being. It puts the Aristotelian formula of a
zoon politicon into practice and makes it possible
to interpret every manifestation of life on the basis
of its social meaning. Adler viewed man as embed-
ded in the community of his fellowman, which furnishes both the resources and the problems of his
life. Adler measured the degree of failure in emotional development by the ethical norm of an ideal
communal life and work that involves a contribution
to the general welfare. He knew that a person can
overcome his fear of life only if he has a stable relationship to his human environment and that a person's all-powerful feeling of inferiority can be as-
suaged only when the voice of the community has
begun to resound within him.

Adler has taught us to regard the human personality as an indivisible whole. Beyond all the re-
flexes, drives, and instincts which some schools try
to put together into an ingenious mosaic, he emphasized the unity of the person. This person is determined neither by his biological constitution nor
by his environment; he is a sovereign and self-de-
termining power which, to be sure, is shaped by
inner and outer influences but essentially utilizes
his "circumstances of life" with a certain measure
of freedom and with a style of his own. Adler dis-
cerned this inner freedom of a person in the for-
ward-looking quality of all manifestations of life; almost all the concepts which he created for an
understanding of these phenomena—such as *Le-
bensplan* (style of life), *Persönlichkeitsideal* (self-

ideal), and *personale Finalität* (personal teleology) —presuppose a human subject that is in a position to define and actualize himself. In rejecting the drive mechanism, Adler gives the human personality the responsibility that belongs to it. Consequently its life-style, which psychoanalysis had delegated to a multiplicity of drives, becomes its very own work; in sickness as in health it is the co-designer of the paths and blind alleys in which its more or less great errors cause it to get stuck.

Adler regarded the evolution of living things as proof that an inextinguishable urge for further development and perfection is active in human beings as well. He regarded the achievements of culture, art, science, and philosophy, as well as the general respect for human life, as products of such a striving for perfection. To him the task of the process of civilization was the social development of man. The current state of social development, the inadequacy of which is evidenced by catastrophes of world historical dimensions, defines the demands of the future, which for Adler can be met only by a growing social interest. Increased ties between one human being and another constitute the basis not only of an individual's happiness but also of the advancement of the community as a whole. Within such a conceptual framework there naturally is no room for a primary antithesis between the individual and society. It is the view of psychoanalysis that social considerations are alien to human nature and that what one is fated to experience in civilization is discontent. To such views Adler opposed his well-founded conviction that the community is the origin and the matrix of the truly creative personality.

This was not intended to gloss over the deplorable conditions of the present or the unwholesome aspects of our existence. Adler recognized the discrepancies of our age and also realized how greatly we are burdened with inadequate and obsolete life-styles and institutions. Hence he warned against misinterpreting "devotion to the community" as an adaptation to existing communities; what is now before us with all its imperfections permits us to divine what is right *sub specie aeternitatis*, where human striving becomes meaningful. This evolutionary goal lies in the human psyche, which desires not the psychoanalytic "pleasure" but this very perfection. The Socratic view that virtue is teachable is confirmed anew by the depth psychology process, which opens the doors to human striving for freedom and perfection, doors that were barred in childhood. Help from without may count on cooperation from within. Adler expressed this in words that are characteristic of him and his image of man: "Man is not evil by nature. No matter what transgressions a person may have committed, led astray by his erroneous view of life, this need not oppress him, for he can change. He is free to be happy and to give pleasure to others."

Personality as a Goal-Directed Unit

The theory of individual psychology is based on the assumption that the personality is a goal-directed unit. This view is based upon biological and psychological considerations. Biology teaches us that even an organism is an indivisible unit; all its functions are aimed at maintaining this wholeness and continually restoring it in the face of the encroachments of the environment. This self-actualization lends meaning to the structure and the function of the organs. Accordingly, all manifestations of life must be regarded as *purposeful*. Causality covers only a secondary aspect of life, namely, its physical and chemical part; the real order of living things is goal-directed, purposive activity, and this can be investigated only from a teleological (purpose-oriented) point of view. Adler's teachings thus emphasize the teleological character of the psychic; life and the psyche can be understood only on the basis of this goal-directedness.

For Adler, the psyche was not a metaphysical entity transferred from supernatural spheres to the "prison of the body"; it was an aspect of life, an "organ of attack, defense, security, or protection." The organism moving in free space and exposed to unforeseeable situations and dangers needs the "psychic organ," with the aid of which it orients itself to its surroundings. Mental life itself is motion, too, an incessant dynamic force that safeguards the organism's existence. The biologically determined goal of adaptation and transcendence is reflected in the psychological realm by constant contact with the environment, and every mental manifestation can be interpreted as if it were aiming at a goal of balance and superiority.

For the human personality this goal takes the form of a *self-ideal*, a guiding idea with which an individual strives to overcome his specific inadequacies. Naturally, there are as many variants as there are people. Each human life generates different goals, and every individual seeks in his unique way to master the shared difficulties of existence. Out of general cultural influences, a realization of organic weaknesses or adequacies, and the influence of the environment and education, each human being fashions for himself *with a certain arbitrariness* a law that governs his life and serves as the framework for his subsequent destiny.

The compulsion to look and plan ahead which informs all mental life gives it the orientation toward

the future that permeates every expressive movement. Each individual, as it were, acts in accordance
with his *attitude* toward life. The "conception of the
world" abstracted from experiences of early childhood includes an individual's opinion of himself
and the world, a kind of comparison between the
strength of his personal equipment and the difficulty of his tasks in life. Understandably, this estimate can frequently be quite erroneous. Irrespective of this, according to Adler, everyone acts in
accordance with the goal he has chosen. The more
inferior a person felt as a child, the more he will be
inclined to equip his self-ideal with an increased
safety factor and to demand more and unattainable
things of the future. This gives rise to life problems
which can hardly ever be solved on the basis of experience. Experiences themselves are evaluated in
the light of the *Leitbild* (ideal) and are usually reworked and reinterpreted "subjectively" until they
seem to confirm the personal guiding line. "Every
person *makes* his experiences"—that is, he arranges
them until they fit the outline of his life.

Accordingly, a deeper understanding of a
human being presupposes an intuitive knowledge
of his goal and an ability to relate his life movements
to it. In this regard individual psychology replaces
explaining psychology with *understanding psychology* (Dilthey). It gives free rein to intuition even
though it, like any science, must have firm rules and
principles. It emphatically postulates, however, that
without the idea of a total personality all physical
manifestations of an individual remain two-dimen-
sional. The way in which a person masters any given
situation can never be interpreted merely on the
basis of an action determined by a situation but only
on the basis of this person's *goal in life*. In Adler's

paradoxical formulation, "When two people do the same thing, it is not the same thing."

Such points of view give rise to a dramatic conception of human life. Psychologically illuminated, a human life is like a well-constructed drama that aims at a fifth act in which the problems of the plot are resolved. This finale is often imaginary, dreamt and fabricated by the psychic function of the imagination. Despite its fictitious character, however, it remains a guidepost in all vicissitudes of life without which a person would surely lose his bearings in life's complexity. Thus the self-ideal resembles the point "from which the earth could be lifted off its hinges" (Archimedes). Of necessity each human must, if he wants to master life, transcend the actuality of the troubles and imperfections of his childhood and formulate his goal and direction. Depending on his impressions and experiences, this mastery can take any of numerous forms, such as transcendence, evasion, retreat, and recourse to others.

In his purposiveness a person uses everything he finds as material and resource. This purposiveness is the real higher authority in man. All organic functions, intelligence, language, and ties to his fellowman are integrated into this "finalism" and are used (if necessary, misused) by it. The anxiety affect, for example, is a biological phenomenon; in neurosis and psychosis it is employed with unconscious purposefulness against the environment as an appeal and a coercion. The entire neurotic symptomatology is comprehensible only when one assumes with Adler that these symptoms are produced meaningfully in order to give the life of an inwardly insecure person the protection of extenuating circumstances. Nor does the fact of inner conflicts contradict the goal-oriented unity of the personality. All the so-called ambivalences (E. Bleuler) as well as Faust's famous "two souls that dwell in one's breast" are, according to Adler, an expression of a "hesitant attitude toward life," which requires inner struggles to evade decisions and take refuge in the feeling of indecision. If a person wavers and doubts, *nothing happens*, and precisely this may be an apparently ambivalent individual's idea of a goal.

In contrast to psychoanalysis, which has split human nature into numerous conflicting drives and tendencies, Adler's teaching is a theory of the autonomous personality, which through its goals and setting of purpose definitely aims at becoming a whole. Only a holistic approach reveals the deeper meaning of the manifestations of life, of which the psychic element is part and substance.

Organ Inferiority, Compensation, and Overcompensation

A medical-biological problem constitutes the point of departure for individual-psychological research. Adler's investigations of the causes of diseases led him to name not only the exogenous factor (such as infection, poisoning, and overwork) but the endogenous one of an original organ inferiority as well. He proceeded from the pathological-anatomical premise that the quality of organs varies a great deal. Along with healthy and fully functioning organs, an organism frequently has organs that must be called "inferior." This inferiority manifests itself in anomalies of location, form, or function. In addition to functional peculiarities it usually means an increased susceptibility to diseases, which tend to attack this place of least resistance.

Adler's *Study of Organ Inferiority* (1907) demonstrates the connection between organ inferiority
and fate in life on the basis of numerous specific
cases. The study also gives careful consideration to
heredity. According to Adler's findings, specific
organ inferiorities are transmissible, and thus it is
possible to trace the susceptibility of a certain organ
or system of organs through whole genealogies. A
primary organ weakness, however, need not always
lead to deficiency symptoms; functional disturbances or illnesses appear only if greater demands
are made on an organism and the inferior organ is
incapable of making the required adjustment.

Organ inferiorities constitute a considerable
burden on the organism affected by them. The
struggle for self-assertion, which starts immediately
after birth, is bound to affect the inferior organ more
strongly and more permanently. The question arises
as to how an organism attempts to cope with these
difficulties. Adler bases his answer on the observation that an organism is capable of compensation.
In its process of growth and development it is able
to compensate for innate or acquired defects. This
thesis is supported by numerous clinical experiences. For example, in valvular heart disease the
myocardium tumefies and in this way ensures the
necessary increased performance. If a kidney is removed, the remaining kidney doubles in size within
a short time and takes over the function of the lost
symmetrical organ. Not infrequently the weakness
of one eye is compensated for by the other eye's
exceptional acuity of vision. In a blind person the
sense of touch and the sense of hearing take over
the function of spatial orientation, and this generally
leads to enhancement of these senses.

According to Adler, inferior organs are, de-

pending on the compensatory capacity of the total
organism, sites of susceptibility to illness, of compensation, or of overcompensation. Under unfavorable conditions they remain below the average functional value for the lifetime of the individual. In
favorable cases the compensatory endeavor does not
stop at the "normal value," and with the aid of an
increased mental effort it leads to a level of performance that normal organs cannot reach. In Adler's earliest teachings this theory of overcompensation constitutes the point of departure for an
understanding of outstanding cultural activity, particularly in the fields of art and science. This compensation for organ insufficiency thus appears as the
bearer of advancing culture. Adler managed to demonstrate that great orators (Demosthenes), compos-
ers (Beethoven, Smetana), painters, and poets suffered from the inferiority of precisely those organs
that they used to achieve perfection in their art.

With these aspects the theory of organ inferiority rises above the purely biological realm and
brings the psychic factors to the fore. On a human
plane, next to the biological evolutionary tendencies described in comprehensive fashion by Darwin
and Lamarck, the outstanding compensatory capacity of the psyche must be considered. In light of its
weakness and infirmity, as well as its deficient supply of natural weapons or tools, the human organism
is itself inferior; only the psychic compensatory efforts of civilization and culture have made it viable
and capable of development. In the life of an individual, too, the *psychic organ* has the important
task of providing the more or less helpless organism
with protection and security. Adler occasionally
uses the expression *psychic superstructure* to indicate that all psychic elements must be understood

as a response and reaction to the biological and social conditions of the struggle for existence.

The theory of organ inferiority throws a new light on the problem of talent, and it is also the real basis of psychosomatic medicine, which developed later. At an early date Adler pointed out that inferior organs tend to lead to childhood disorders (such as bed-wetting, digestive disturbances, and stuttering) and that they can easily become part of emotional shocks. Since every affective state always has its physical counterpart (e.g., sweating, diarrhea, trembling with fear), it is not surprising that prolonged emotional tension should disturb the functioning of an organism and draw attention to any inferior organs. In such cases the neurotic psyche expresses itself through the inferior organ—in an "organ dialect," as it were, which gives a physical demonstration of the emotional irritation. Adler's presentation of the psychogenesis of such disturbances anticipated many things that present-day psychosomatic medicine sometimes explains in more roundabout fashion—because it has not always adopted Adler's coherent view.

The theory of organ inferiority is one of the pillars of individual psychology. Even though Adler's late concepts went far beyond his early formulations, this part of his system occupies a key position in the whole, and its significance must not be underestimated.

The Feeling of Inferiority

Inferiority feeling and *inferiority complex* are the most popular concepts of individual psychology which have become part of everyday linguistic usage. These terms coined by Adler have numerous

precursors in intellectual history, of which we shall
mention only those of Stendhal (*sentiment d'infér-
iorité*) and Janet (*sentiment d'incomplétude*). But
only in Adler's description do these phenomena
gain their real depth and significance, which can
become apparent only against the background of the
entire theory of individual psychology. Those psychological schools that have torn Adler's findings
out of their context and reinterpreted them by
means of a different terminology usually have also
lost sight of the basic substance of these findings.
Thus the *castration complex* of the psychoanalysts
is an obvious imitation of the inferiority complex of
individual psychology; though it has been trans-
muted into the sexual jargon and thus brought closer
to the preconceived theory, it has been largely al-
ienated from life.

According to Adler, the feeling of inferiority is
one of the most important facts of human mental life.
It is not an accidental and incidental phenomenon
but is virtually anchored in human nature. Man is
the only creature that has been deprived of nearly
all natural weapons and aids. His situation in nature
is characterized by a general inadequacy; he is an
insufficient creature, who must laboriously produce
all his own advantages and assets. Culture and civilization encompass the history of man's efforts to
control his imperfections. He would never have
been able to start the triumphant advance of his
technical and scientific development if the eternal
goad of his inadequate physical constitution had not
been active in his psyche. In this sense we owe to
man's existential angst (that is, his inferiority feeling) his continual striving for transcendence, which
has given rise to all great achievements in the development of mankind.

Who can seriously doubt that the human individual, to whom nature has been so unkind, has been given the blessing of a strong feeling of inferiority which strives for a positive situation, for security, transcendence? . . . A long time ago I emphasized that to be human means to feel inferior . . . The feeling of inferiority dominates our mental life and can be easily understood on the basis of an individual's and mankind's feeling of imperfection and incompleteness, of their constant striving.

(Adler, *Der Sinn des Lebens*).

This universal human feeling of inferiority is aroused anew in every infant and young child, and it is a spur to growth and development. By reason of his very smallness and helplessness a child must gain the impression that he is hardly fit to live. Under favorable conditions the child is not discouraged by this but initiates psychic movements that are intended to let him transcend this feeling of inadequacy. All growth and development come under the influence of this tendency and act as a tireless spur to the innumerable learning processes in which the child does an enormous amount of work in the course of a few years. Adler also traces the *educability* of a child to his inferiority feeling. His very weakness means that the child needs support, and it makes him willing to cooperate with the educational endeavor—provided that pedagogical incompetence does not force him to compensate for his existential angst by being a stubborn and problem child.

A feeling of inferiority becomes an impediment to development only if the child is fixated in it and finds no way out of his situation. Then his pessimism and his timidity consolidate into an *inferiority complex*, which is already in the realm of emotional pathology. This produces a standstill in the psychic

movement; the child cannot grow out of his perceived insufficiency and tries pseudocompensa-
tions by means of which he seeks to subjugate his
environment. Every inferiority complex contains a
clear admonition to the environment on which demands are made and which is exploited. This leads
to a struggle on the *uselessness side of life* and to a
refusal to integrate, which bring about psychoneu-
rosis in all its manifestations.

An inferiority complex can develop on the basis
of numerous conditions. As Adler emphasized in his
Theory of Organ Inferiority, organic defects frequently give rise to heightened feelings of inferiority. Perceived organic weaknesses of all kinds—
homeliness, red hair, nearsightedness, lefthanded-
ness, etc.—can demonstrate a child's inadequacy to
him in quite drastic fashion, and this can become
the source of a permanent feeling of weakness. Here
the physical facts are less significant than the way
in which the child sees and utilizes them. That is
why even minor organic defects can produce grave
psychological consequences.

The social and economic situation of a child
must also be mentioned here. Adler has repeatedly
pointed out that poverty and need give the growing
child a pessimistic picture of his situation in life and
of his future possibilities. In general, we find deeper
despondency among workingmen's children than
among children from the middle class. It should be
society's duty to moderate the social differences, so
that no child has to grow up with the stigma of deprivation.

Gender is another aspect that illuminates the
origin of the inferiority complex. Individual psychology has identified male supremacy in patriarchal civilization as the cause of a prevalent female
feeling of inferiority. According to Adler, a woman

finds it difficult to cope with her female role in a world determined by men. The differences in the valuation of the two sexes that are based on mythological preconceptions result in combative feelings, which come together in the so-called masculine protest. Thus both a man and a woman can come under the spell of the statement "I want to be a real man," a slogan that compulsively extends to all manifestations of life.

Position within the family can also become a cause of an inferiority complex. Thus an only child, the youngest child, the child displaced as the center of attention by a new sibling, the only girl among boys, or the only boy among girls may run the risk of developing, on the basis of this position, a narrowminded view of life that will impede his or her further development.

Education, finally, is the most important factor in the origin of marked feelings of inferiority. All the other factors mentioned above are such that their pathological significance can be neutralized by a sympathetic education. In a certain sense there is nothing that could compel a person to develop an inferiority complex. All handicaps of an organic, social, or familial nature can be largely compensated for by pedagogical skill and psychological sensitivity. If education does not do its job, however, it can produce the gravest failures even under the most favorable outward circumstances. The educational methods of coddling on the one hand and toughness and strictness on the other are particularly to blame for failures in emotional development. In both modes a child fails to learn to compensate for his helplessness by means of growing social ties; in both educational situations the world is bound to appear hostile to him and stifle his creative energy.

Inferiority feeling and inferiority complex are

the "red thread" that runs through the entire mental pathology. The nervous or "untalented" child, the emotionally unbalanced adult, the neurotic, the criminal, the pervert, the mental patient—all are permeated by the feeling of their own inadequacy, against which they desperately try to rebel. This gives rise to a psychic striving designed to put a stop to their anxiety and their insufficiency. According to Adler, this is the *striving for superiority* or the will to power, which in both mental health and mental illness undertakes the task of overcoming a perceived weakness or curtailment.

Striving for Superiority and Will to Power

In superficial presentations Adler's teaching occasionally is characterized as a "psychology of the striving for power." This simplification completely misses the point of individual psychology; it is no more than a catchword that is, for the most part, used derogatorily. In reality Adler never placed the will to power at the center of his teachings. The striving for power and superiority was to him one expression of human psychic life, in conflict with other tendencies, such as social interest, which have an even wider significance.

Adler's essay "The Aggression Drive in Life and Neurosis" (1908; reprinted in *Heilen und Bilden*, 1914) may have contributed to the erroneous view of individual psychology. In this brief study Adler postulates a primary aggression drive, which is already active in a child and which tries to cope with reality by a certain hostility. This striving is said to intertwine with the other drives, such as sexuality and visual, auditory, and motor readinesses, in such a way that every manifestation of life comprises a combination of aggressiveness with other driving forces. But this essay already emphasizes that "the social interest innate in man must be regarded as the most important regulator of the aggression drive."

Soon thereafter Adler abandoned this point of view, which was later taken up by Freud and incorporated into the cheerless theory of the *death instinct*. The only alternative this theory sees for man is that between self-destruction and destruction of the environment. It burdens human nature with an ineradicable tendency toward destruction and ends with the resigned observation that death is the meaning and goal of all life.

The striving for superiority, which in Adler's later theories represents the function of the *aggression drive*, is not a drive and thus not a natural component of the human psyche. It is a secondary phenomenon which arises as a consequence of the primary feeling of inferiority. In emotional life the latter gives rise to the urge to set a goal for oneself in which every perceived insecurity appears to be compensated for. In Adler's view, the same compensation mechanism which he has described for inferior organs also guides psychic activity. Here, too, everything strives for compensation of weaknesses and inadequacies, and when there are stronger feelings of inferiority one must expect attempts at *overcompensation* which are not content with an average measure of security. The "*psychic organ*" tries to escape from the deficient self-assessment in childhood by means of more vigorous and more wide-ranging movements. This leads to the development of a heightened and exaggerated striving for power and superiority, one that can assume pathological forms.

Thus the goal of superiority is a response to a feeling of inferiority and constitutes its exact counterpart. It can assume as many forms as there are people. It is striven for overtly and covertly, and an individual is aware or unaware of it to varying degrees. Not infrequently it is disguised as its opposite, namely, social interest, and thus it craftily misuses the credulity and social interest of others for its own asocial purposes.

The most appropriate compensation for a feeling of insecurity lies in an urge for growth and in a striving to acquire knowledge, ability, and skills. Thus the educational and learning process is also based on a striving for superiority, and hardly anyone will object to that. In the imitation of adults, in children's games, in daydreams and nocturnal dreams, every child fantasizes about a future in which he expects greatness and recognition. As long as these fantasies remain on the level of the common good and of development for communal life and cooperation, there is room for a person's superiority, which need not bring him in conflict with his environment.

A person's character also reflects the ever-present amalgam of social interest with striving for superiority. As we shall show more systematically later, all *active* character traits—ambition, vanity, envy, avarice, hatred, etc.—contain a direct expression of the striving for superiority. If a person fails in his pursuit of his overt will to power, there is a deviation into an indirect manifestation, and then the same superiority ideals can be striven for by *passive* means. To an observer trained in individual psychology, seemingly nonaggressive characteristics—including submissiveness, lack of independence, laziness, masochism, obedience—are revealed as tricky methods of attaining dominance by demonstrating weakness or tractability.

Such mechanisms must be regarded as part of all failures in emotional development. When tempted by some external or internal influences, even a child can exert his superiority and power in compelling his parents to pay attention to him. To reach this goal the child may neglect his further development and retain bad habits or childhood disorders in order thereby to defy his environment and its educational efforts. Anxiety, shyness, and symptoms of all kinds are a clear warning to the parents to give more attention to the child; these place the social interest of the environment in the service of an illusory superiority roughly in keeping with the formula: I am weaker, more vulnerable, and more in need of help than the others.

The goal of superiority is incomprehensible to most people, and it is beyond the self-knowledge of the average person, who can name various personal qualities or defects but hardly ever in the right proportion. This is due to the fact that every person's ideal of personality originates at an age when his linguistic tools are imperfectly developed; hence the will to superiority is not given verbal expression and the individual has an obscure idea of it without this idea assuming an enduring form. In this connection Adler speaks of an *unconscious fiction*; this expression originates in Hans Vaihinger's philosophy of "As If" [*Als Ob*] which proceeds from the assumption that human perceptual activity operates with false but usable auxiliary constructs that permit an orientation in the chaos of life. For example, geography draws over the surface of the earth, which is essentially indivisible, a grid of meridians that yield a meaningful division and make it possible to measure the location of every place. Similarly, the human psyche must also draw guidelines in the incalculable realm of its possibilities, and of these the guideline of power and superiority seems to promise the overcoming of dangers.

All psychic illnesses—nervousness, neurosis, criminality, perversion, psychosis—are dictated by the striving for superiority and more or less clearly display a tendency to dominate the environment by fictive means (in the sense of "As If"). In neurosis, according to Adler, we see a diminution of the living space, which is all the more dramatically dominated and shaken up with the aid of the neurotic symptoms. In perversion, love is degraded and transformed into a power struggle in which all possibilities of debasement and retreat can be exploited. Criminality proves to be a struggle against society, having the aim of enrichment at the cost of others or of ruthlessly making one's way through the destruction of human lives. Finally, in psychosis the striving for godlikeness manifests itself in drastic and undisguised fashion. Delusional ideas are exemplifications of the theory of individual psychology which ought to give pause even to a prejudiced observer.

To some critics of individual psychology it is a puzzle how human beings can, for the sake of the "bubble" of their striving for superiority, bring themselves to endure the suffering and the sorrow that any neurotic illness involves for the person afflicted with it. Yet one must clearly realize that it is a universally human habit to chase after phantoms and to fool oneself and others. In politics, religion, and everyday life the *will to illusion* and the *life lie* are also triumphant. The neurosis of an individual hardly differs from the neurosis of society as a whole. The reason why it is so hard to recognize is that everyone swims along in the stream of this neurotic civilization, where an erroneous response to

the questions of life is the rule and sound and progressive attempts at solution are the exception. A
neurotic is a *prestige politician* like everyone else.
That he strays from reality a bit more than a so-called
normal person is due to the overburdening impressions and experiences of his childhood, which sug-
gested to him a retreat from social reality. In his
book *Being and Nothingness* Sartre presents many
analogous insights. He writes: "Man is a failed attempt to become God." Adler would have readily
endorsed this, particularly as far as his psychopathology was concerned.

In Adler's last works the striving for superiority
is given a new foundation. The evolutionary viewpoint comes even more clearly to the fore, and since
according to Adler all living things harbor an urge
for perfection, the will to power is also shored up
by this motive. Under the pressure of familial and
cultural conditions the misled striving for perfection, which awakens in every child as a gift of human
development, is pressed into the pattern of personal
superiority, a trait which civilization has nurtured
for thousands of years through its unbounded ven-
eration of martial heroism, covetousness, and male
superiority over women. This way of solving the existential questions of mankind seemed obsolete to
Adler. For the safeguarding of evolution he demanded a deepening and widening of *social interest*, and he believed the future of humanity to be
dependent on the furtherance of this concept.

Social Interest

The theory of social interest is the keystone of
individual psychology. All other findings must be
related to this central concept if they are to be
understood in any deeper sense. More than any

other branch of depth psychology, Adler's individual psychology borders on sociology at this point. It
views man as a social being and as a matter of principle interprets all phenomena of life as interpersonal interactions. Only with this key can the riddle
of emotional life be unraveled. Fellowship is the
basic structure of human existence.

At first Adler attempted to present social interest as a biological fact. He pointed out that, like all
more highly organized living creatures, man has always lived in communities. Only by banding together did he succeed in overcoming his helplessness in the face of all-powerful nature. Without a
community organization mankind would never have
been able to preserve itself. The biological weakness of human beings makes societal protection necessary. All achievements of civilization have grown
on the soil of community living. Language, the use
of tools, and conceptual thinking are results of social
evolution, and it has created almost everything that
constitutes the foundation of our present life. Only
on the basis of community tradition has cultural
progress been possible.

According to Adler, this situation of man has a
correspondence in a psychological compulsion to
form communities, which expresses itself in an *innate social interest*. This all-powerful striving is, as
it were, anchored in the psychic structure as an inextinguishable disposition. It is not, however, a matter
of an *instinct* which can overcome any resistance
with natural power. The form and shape which social interest assumes in a person depends primarily
on his impressions in childhood and youth. Experience has taught us that the degree of fellow feeling
developed by an individual can vary from a minimal
amount in the case of psychological failures to the
point of genius, which can give new directions to

mankind through its strongest rootedness in community life.

According to Adler, social interest begins to develop with the relationship between mother and
child. In contrast to psychoanalysis, which speaks
of a "parasitism" of the child and describes sucking
on the mother's breast in sadistic terms, Adler views
the relationship between a mother and her child as
a symbiosis which has a beneficial influence on
both. Only in the first weeks of life does a child
primarily take and receive; with the very first smile
a contact with fellow human beings is established,
and as the child's abilities grow, this increasingly
becomes an exchange of feelings. From these conditions it can be seen that a mother's love is one of
the greatest and most decisive sources of social interest. By virtue of the fact that the mother teaches
the child to cooperate for the first time in his life,
she stands at the entrance to fellow feeling generally. The fateful influence which she necessarily exerts on the child demands an appropriate preparation of the mother for her task, a task in which the
foundation of civilization is laid. According to Adler,
the mother must not only arouse social interest in
the child, but she must also promote its extension
to the other members of the family. Individual psychology has observed that pampered children in
particular are in danger of having their social interest fixated on the person who pampers them and to
regard life as a symbiosis with that person. Fellow
feeling in the real sense, however, requires that the
child's upbringing give him the courage to reach out
beyond the family with his feelings and to take an
interest in questions of friendship, love, culture, and
humanity.

Adler pointed out that the suppression of and
disdain for women in patriarchal-authoritarian cul-

tures usually also destroys their self-esteem. This
has a direct and indirect effect on what happens in
education. Women who are unhappy, despondent,
or malcontent will hardly do justice to their pedagogical function. The development of the female
personality, which has been impeded for thousands
of years, is indispensable for evolving human civilization. Only an emotionally healthy mother will
be able to raise happy children.

But it cannot be overlooked that the inclination toward
cooperation is stimulated from the first day. The enormous significance of the mother in this respect is clearly
evident. The mother is at the threshold of the development of social interest. The biological heritage of human
social interest awaits her care. With little acts of assist-
ance—in the bath and in all ministrations the helpless
child needs—she can strengthen or impede the child's
contact. Her relationship with the child, her understanding, and her skill are influential means . . . It is safe to
say that the contact with the mother is of the greatest significance for the development of social interest in a
human being. If we had to do without this all-powerful
lever in the development of mankind, we would be hard
put to find a half-way adequate substitute, quite apart
from the fact that the maternal feeling of contact would
resist destruction as an inalienable property of evolution.
We probably owe to this maternal feeling the major por-
tion of human social feeling, and with it the essential existence of human civilization.

Also, it is always important for the child to learn
to include his father and his siblings in his growing
social interest. If the mother ties the child to her to
an inordinate degree, she impedes this development. Pampering mothers and harsh fathers create
that artificial psychic product which Freud has described as an Oedipus complex. But even with such
faulty upbringing a child will hardly go so far as to

desire to possess his mother sexually and to kill his father. For Adler the entire problem of the Oedipal situation boils down to the question of a child's pampering.

Like feelings of inferiority and the striving for superiority, social interest also receives its characteristic stamp in the early years of life and becomes an unconscious, relatively constant part of the personality, which as a rule can be significantly enhanced only through psychotherapy or similarly far-reaching processes of consciousness. Thus a person's readiness to cooperate can remain unchanged throughout his life even if a thousand experiences seem to push him beyond the limitations of his childhood—a fact that remains incomprehensible if one overlooks the molding power of childhood impressions.

How can one recognize the social interest or the degree of fellow feeling in a person? It is, of course, not a matter of the words with which that person embraces the community and avows communal values; only his actions can reveal his mentality. According to Adler, a person's attitude toward his tasks in life, tasks that are always social in nature and require a developed social interest for their stable and satisfactory solution, is a sure indication of the extent to which a person is ready to lead his life as a social human being.

In his systematic work *Individualpsychologie* (1928), Erwin Wexberg points out some meanings of the concept *Gemeinschaftsgefühl* (social interest) which reveal the comprehensive content of this fundamental idea. According to Wexberg, genuine fellow feeling is manifested in the following:

1. *Objectivity.* Only a person with *Mitmenschlichkeit* (fellow feeling) is capable of remaining

objective and of letting the matter take precedence over the person.

2. *Logical thinking.* This results only from courage
to investigate the facts consistently, irrespective
of egotistical prejudices and wishful thinking
that constrict one's vision.

3. *Readiness to contribute.* A person with fellow
feeling is willing to do his share for the common
welfare and through his contribution to guarantee the existence and the further development of
the community.

4. *Readiness for devotion to nature and art.* Social
interest, if it is present, cannot stop at the extra-
human world, and it manifests itself in interre-
lationships with life and the universe as well as
with the creations of art, in which human feeling
presents itself in sublime form.

5. *Responsibility for actions, ideas, feelings, etc.* A
person with fellow feeling knows he is responsible for the form of his life, and he assumes responsibility for everything that falls within the
range of his knowledge and ability.

Wexberg's formal descriptions give only a faint
impression of Adler's theory of social interest. In
Adler's late writings, fellow feeling is described as
the real meaning of life. It is human reality as much
as it is a cultural ideal. It is the only thing that can
be expected to guarantee the continued existence
of civilization and human happiness, while its ad-
versary, the striving for power, leads to man's downfall and doom. In 1919 Adler wrote in his foreword
to the second edition of his book *Über den nervösen
Charakter*:

Between the two editions of this book there was the World
War with its continuations; there was the most horrible
mass neurosis which our neurotic civilization, corroded
by its striving for power and its prestige politics, has

willed into being. The horrendous course of events is a terrible confirmation of the simple thoughts contained in this book, and it reveals itself to be the demonic work of the generally unleashed lust for power, which is smothering or craftily abusing the immortal social interest of mankind. Our individual psychology has progressed far beyond dead center. To view and know a human being in our spirit means to wrest him from the aberrations of his hurt, whipped-up, but impotent striving for godlikeness and to make him disposed toward the unshakable logic of human communal living, *social interest.*

Only unsympathetic observers in whom there is little fellow feeling will confuse Adler's teaching with an apologia for a herd existence and adduce a banal individualism in opposition to it. Still others misinterpret Adler's "society" as some actual social order to which they wish to adapt the individual. In the face of this Adler emphasized in his last works that genuine social interest is oriented toward an ideal society of the future. This is a kind of transcendental idea, a guiding star pointing to all that seems right for human beings and humanity. Adler was modest enough to speak here of a presentiment which those conscious of values can have if they are permeated by fellow feeling: "The question of the right way seems solved to me, even though we often grope in the dark. We will not make any decisions, but we can say only one thing: We can regard an individual movement and a mass movement as valuable only if it creates values for eternity, for the higher development of mankind."

(From *Der Sinn des Lebens* [*Social Interest: A Challenge to Mankind*]).

The Three Tasks of Life

Social interest is required for the solution of all tasks of life because these are always social in structure and presuppose fellow feeling. Adler viewed all of human life from the vantage point of answers to questions growing out of communality. These arise from man's situation on earth. The difficulties faced by everyone are related to the cosmic and social conditions on which the human world is based. To the same degree to which a person is rooted in this world will he be capable of making his contribution to the community. Only in this way will he safeguard his mental health and place himself in the mainstream of evolution, whose heir and continuator he is.

It is due to the deficient social development presently attained by man that he can easily stray from this path and attempt to find unsuitable answers to the questions of life. For individual psychology this is not an occasion for moral observations but simply an indication of the extent to which a person has been prepared in his childhood for the problems of communal living. From a person's youthful impressions we can understand why he can muster only partial solutions to his life's problems and why and where he changes course in order to escape the dangers of a personal defeat or a diminution in values (which often is only imagined).

As already mentioned, a child's symbiosis with his mother is a social task which, in its elaboration, permits of all sorts of inadequacies. Success or failure in this relationship usually reveals itself unmistakably in how the child relates to the other members of the family. As in a test, pampering by the mother will be shown by a deficient ability on the part of the child to form attachments and frequently also by a diminished readiness to accommodate himself to a social function of his organs, such as cleanliness and proper speech.

In kindergarten and in school the growing child enters a larger communal field, in which his fellow feeling is constantly tested. The child faces playing, learning, comradeship, and integration into the community of his class as new tasks, which he will complete courageously and cooperatively only if his preparation in the bosom of his family has not caused him to falter. All of a child's modes of behavior which burden his school life and impede the progress of his development—timidity, mendacity, lack of concentration, little desire to learn, usually also apparent lack of talent—are, from the viewpoint of individual psychology, movements of escape from the menacingly approaching life front which children afflicted with a faulty upbringing feel they cannot cope with. As a rule, the intellectual failures are consequences of emotional inadequacy deriving from a disturbed feeling of one's own value and a diminished social interest. Hence individual psychology assigns to the school the task not only of conveying information but also of giving pride of place to the development of a child's personality. We shall elaborate on this later.

Puberty and the awakening of the sexual drive are further burdens which accurately test the strength of an adolescent's fellow feeling. There is no doubt that this period in human life brings upheavals and a widening of the horizon in equal measure. But the way in which a young person enters this new territory or shrinks back from it is characteristic of the guidelines acquired in his childhood. Neglect, juvenile delinquency, dementia praecox, and/or suicide may be in store for those who have not learned to cooperate at an earlier age and whom a greater measure of freedom and energy now causes to demonstrate their error more drastically.

According to Adler, for a growing person the problems of life take the definitive form of work, love, and fellow feeling. The last-named is the most comprehensive, encompassing the other two. Individual psychology judges a person by his solution of these ineluctable questions of human existence. In all emotional failures it can demonstrate that those who feel timid and inferior evade these questions and put partial answers in place of the required wholeness.

The *task of work* arises from the natural conditions of human existence. Only a contribution by everyone guarantees the continued existence of mankind. In pursuing some useful occupation a person does his share for the general welfare at the same time that he fulfills himself in the feeling of performing a productive activity. A person's *work character* is, as a rule, characteristic of his general attitude; it, too, is an indication of "the individual tenor of a person, his character" (Wexberg, p. 85).

The *task of love* is determined by the fact that nature has provided two sexes and thus created the demand for union with a sexual partner. In the union of the two sexes lies the strongest feeling of happiness that life can bestow; it is only through the communion between the I and the Thou and the surrender inherent in it that a person discovers his own self and his real nature. Only a developed fellow feeling can properly accomplish this task. "It is as though each of these persons must forget himself completely and fully surrender to the other person to do justice to the problem of love, as if one being must be formed out of two people." Here, too, a faulty life movement, such as the anxiety-ridden orientation toward personal superiority, will lead to myriad forms of degeneration, which of necessity carry in their train discontent and misfortune.

As already indicated, work and love are *questions of community*. They arise from a circumstance emphasized by individual psychology—namely, that man is a social being and that all his problems are social in nature. Hence, in addition to useful occupation and love, this rubric includes interest in questions of a larger context, problems of cities and countries, nations and mankind. One's relationship to nature and to art is also suffused with communal spirit and will lead to universally useful solutions only if the person turning to these forces of life does not deny his fellow feeling. Informed persons will observe that many people seek in their love of nature and enthusiasm for the arts only an asylum for their neuroses, a refuge in which they hope to find relief from the problems of life, and thus they never get beyond sterility and pseudoachievement.

The problems of life are not a diagnostic invention of individual psychology but conditions of real life on which a person cannot avoid taking a stand. The way in which a person copes with them—whether he overcomes them, is defeated by them, or contents himself with inadequate attempts to solve them—gives us an *index of his mental health* that is better than any test results, even those from the most ingenious testing situations. Such findings are anything but accidental, and moreover they permit us to predict the future, since individual psychology has recognized that the *style of life* remains relatively constant (unless psychotherapy alters it by influencing it systematically). For Adler the tasks of life constitute a normative element; they unfailingly indicate the extent to which social feeling has been developed in each individual. And herein lies the only "world court" that we know if we remain within the sphere of science: "With some experience and calm, sympathetic reflection everyone is likely to realize that the degree of our social interest is constantly tested by means of the problems of life and that we are recognized or rejected on this basis." (*Der Sinn des Lebens*, p. 44).

The Meaning of Life

In Adler's view, it is the task of psychology to show people the true meaning of life. In this it occasionally borders on philosophy and expands its factual knowledge into a comprehensive view of life. Individual psychology is capable of setting up criteria for stable life values. Only from this perspective is it also in a position to show an individual the way to overcome the entanglements of his anxieties and feelings of inferiority in which he is caught up.

Adler's philosophy follows the ideas of evolutionism. The present structure of our life derives from the fact of the evolution of living things. But the problems and predicaments on which we founder are transitional stages of the development which living creatures go through by dint of their inherent urge for perfection. In life itself there resides a creative energy which has led from the protozoa to Homo sapiens and in human beings works toward ever better emotional and intellectual development and productive power. The goal of this development is determined by the relationship between life and the environment. The dangers of the constantly changing outer world irresistibly compel new efforts at adaptation, and only those can prove useful which produce a certain harmony with the environment.

Within this overall structure every human life is an attempt to give a meaningful answer to the ineluctable questions of our existence. Love, work, and fellow feeling mark the area within which each individual tries to prove his worth and find fulfillment. The extent to which in these efforts the human striving for perfection is thwarted and impeded by the misguided striving for personal superiority determines the value of the resulting solutions. All human failures are on the level of a deficiently developed social interest and a morbidly heightened striving for superiority. In its impotent resignation this striving substitutes for contributions to the community all kinds of failures: neurotic symptoms, criminal acts, psychotic confusion, and innumerable character deformations.

According to the impression made by one's childhood experiences, the goal of perfection appears to everyone in a different form and shape. Like a healthy person, an emotionally ill person has an evolutionary urge, which differs in that this urge is farther removed from truth and reality as determined by communal life. In Adler's modest formulation, it is only the "lesser error" that separates the healthy and the sick. Even the teachings of individual psychology appeared to him as a provisional attempt to gain an orientation to human life. Since no one is blessed with absolute truth, science, too, can only approximate it, though it offers the best and most serviceable approach to it that man can muster.

Accordingly, the meaning of life for a person can reside only in his attainment of the greatest possible harmony with his human environment and with the universe. This demand contains not only the idea of an adaptation but also an appeal to an evolutionary upward movement on which the weal and woe of humankind depend. For Adler there was no doubt that such a development had to include above all an intensification of human social interest. "I would regard any current as justified whose orientation provides irrefutable proof that its guiding aim is the welfare of all of mankind. I would regard any current as misguided which runs counter to this viewpoint or is informed by the Cain-like formula 'Why should I love my neighbor'?"

Naturally, the *common welfare* is a concept that permits of many interpretations. With this alleged aim the greatest crimes of human history have been committed. That is why Adler was always careful to endow this formal direction with substantial meaning. By espousing socialist humanism and placing nonviolence at the center of his teachings, he made it clear that he viewed the common welfare as founded only on an overcoming of the rule of castes and classes, the abolition of any moral and material coercion, and the absolute equality of "everything with a human countenance." The community in which he wanted to see a person settled is not the ordinary community of the here and now, which shows all the defects of transition, but the ideal community of the future, which it is the meaning of civilization to strive for. Everything that resists this evolving human community is condemned to perform the paltry function of a drag which is overcome—and forgotten—by the forward-moving development. As we have already seen:

This fact becomes even more convincing and perhaps even more self-evident when we ask what happened to those people who contributed nothing to the common good. The answer is that they have completely vanished. Not a trace of them has remained; they have become physically and spiritually extinct. Their fate was that of extinct species of animals which were unable to live in harmony with the cosmic realities. Actually, a secret law is at work here. It is as if the questioning cosmos commanded: Away with you! You have not grasped the meaning of life. You cannot extend into the future.

Militarism and war, authoritarian education, disdain for women, economic disadvantaging of the masses of the people, religious and national intolerance—all these are forms of community living in which the deleterious spirit of violence blocks the path of the growing social interest. The erring individual only reflects an erring humanity beset by deficient social development. Adler's hope was directed at freeing the stifled social interest from the limitations of individual and social life and to enhance the courage, productivity, and happiness of people by increasing their knowledge of human nature. In the midst of the horrors of his time and the eruption of fascist barbarism, his optimism and his kindliness kept him from succumbing to resignation. This was his creed:

There is reason to expect that at a much later date, if mankind has enough time left, the power of social interest will overcome all external resistance. Then people will express social interest as naturally as they breathe. Until that time comes, probably the only thing to do is to understand this necessary course of things and to teach it.

3

Individual Psychology and Holistic Theory

The individual psychology of Alfred Adler has some basic concepts which one can easily adopt without reflecting on their deeper significance. Thus the terms *Minderwertigkeitsgefühl* (feeling of inferiority), *Geltungsstreben* (striving for superiority), and *Gemeinschaftsgefühl* (social interest) have become common in psychological terminology and everyday parlance, but even a professional psychologist will have a hard time giving an exact definition of what he means by these terms. It is not easy to supply such a clear definition. To be sure, Adler's psychology is regarded as simple and uncomplicated, but upon closer observation it turns out to be an extremely differentiated theory, which can hardly be properly understood without an extensive knowledge of psychology.

Which of the above-mentioned three concepts is the central one in Adler's teachings? Surely the feeling of inferiority would come to mind first; this term is one almost everyone is conscious of. The inferiority complex has become a symbol of individual psychology, just as the Oedipus complex has become a shibboleth of psychoanalysis. This concept, incidentally, is not completely Adler's intellectual property; long before him it was used by Stendhal, Dostoievsky, and Pierre Janet, at least in the general sense of the term. Adler, to be sure, placed it in the service of psychopathology and of everyday life in an astonishing manner. His statement "To be human means to have feelings of inferiority" must not, however, be interpreted to mean that this is the main force in emotional life. Feelings of inadequacy are one component of the human psyche, not its central feature.

In popular presentations, individual psychology frequently appears as the "doctrine of striving for power" and thus is differentiated from psychology, which supposedly is a "doctrine of the sex drive." Adler frequently and vainly objected to this naive simplification. The *striving for power* is not a "natural constant" in human psychic life. It primarily appears as a compensation for oppressive feelings of inferiority and anxiety; its real goal is not necessarily predominance over others but, rather, security and freedom from fear. The power tendency is instilled in a person by our unfortunate education and culture. It is a mistake to assume that we are dealing with primary natural impulses. Certainly, in all psychopathological states the need for recognition (*Geltungsbedürfnis*) is paramount (on the uselessness side of life), but it is advisable not to attribute such strivings stemming from psychic need to what is called human nature. This distinguishes Adler's views from similar-sounding views of Thomas Hobbes, Friedrich Nietzsche, Stendhal, Dostoievsky, and others. Adler would surely have declined to characterize individual psychology as a psychology of the urge for power.

Adler always regarded *social interest*, something that is basic to all psychic manifestations of life from the very beginning, as more important than the two above-mentioned fundamental forces of emotional life. According to Adler, man is an out-

and-out social creature, and all his psychic functions are related to his feeling of fellowship. Every person wants to be recognized by others; he harbors no inherent tendencies (such as aggression) that would basically prevent him from living and working with others. Hence it is advisable to examine emotional health and illness with reference to the development or the lack of socially oriented endeavors. Only someone who has learned in childhood to combine his own well-being with that of the persons he relates to (and, in the final analysis, these include all of mankind) will be able to lead a happy and productive life. Then, too, the therapy of individual psychology is definitely oriented toward reactivating in a patient the social interest that was smothered by faulty social relationships in early childhood. It is, to be sure, rather difficult to define what social interest or fellow feeling ought to be in concrete cases. As we know, people have very divergent notions about what benefits or harms the community. An unmistakable demonstration of Adler's concept of a "genuine social connectedness" would require a philosophical discussion. This is not the place for it, because we would have to adduce reflections from ethics, philosophical anthropology, and social philosophy.

The foregoing discussion seems to indicate, however, that individual psychology as a theory rests on three pillars: feeling of inferiority, striving for superiority, and social interest. This, at any rate, is what we find in the numerous publications of adherents and of knowledgeable opponents of this doctrine. But does this really express the essence of Adler's overall concept? Our answer would be a definite no, for in our view individual psychology is first and foremost a *holistic theory of emotional life*. It can be best understood if one proceeds from the fact that it brings out the unity and indivisibility of the human personality with particular emphasis. Adler related his theory to the *Individuum* (individual), thus according to this word's literal meaning in Latin, to something indivisible. To understand a person always means to empathize with his unique, unmistakable nature. This holistic thesis recurs everywhere in individual psychology; hence it can hardly be overestimated. In the following remarks we shall endeavor to recognize the idea of *wholeness* in its importance to biology, psychology, psychotherapy, and intellectual history.

In its consideration of the holistic concept, science transcends its customary realm and makes use of metaphysical reflections. *Wholeness* is not simply an empirical finding; it is an idea to which we bring our empirical material so as to put it in order and understand it. But no one can stringently prove that life, consciousness, and personality are necessarily totalities; it is entirely possible to describe biological, psychological, and intellectual facts without the concept of totality. Thus, for example, in psychology and psychotherapy the behaviorists and the behavior therapists can easily reject all ideas of wholeness. These confine themselves to the visible behavior of a person which they want to investigate and perhaps change; that there is a person behind these modes of behavior is vigorously denied by these schools (which base themselves on Watson, Pavlov, and others). Nevertheless, in our estimation depth psychology cannot do without the idea of *personality*; it simply must realize that it is not expressing a scientific insight but a philosophical conviction.

And yet there is much evidence that the thesis of wholeness cannot be a mere delusion for biology, psychology, and all cultural sciences. As we know, the above-mentioned disciplines have represented this view with very convincing arguments, particularly since the turn of the century. Hans Driesch's observation that wholeness (*entelechy* in the Aristotelian sense) to a large extent regulates and determines the vital functions was a turning point in research in the natural sciences. Driesch's experiment with sea urchin eggs became famous; he managed to cut such eggs by means of a loop made of hair, and it became apparent that the two halves of each egg gave rise to two whole, though smaller, sea urchins. This fact was interpreted as an indication that all mechanical explanations of vital processes fall short; one must assess the physical and chemical processes in an organism as being integrated into the *striving for wholeness*. From this insight Driesch derived the justification for a modern *vitalism*, but this is something we cannot discuss in the present context.

The experiences of everyday life also give us many indications of the holistic nature of vital phenomena. For example, if a person is injured (as when a man cuts himself while shaving), the entire organism works toward preserving the integrity of the whole. The multifarious processes necessary for the coagulation of the blood, the healing of the wound, and the formation of a scar are a marvel of cooperative biological functions. It is similar with infectious diseases; the way in which the body customarily copes with pathogens can only be understood as a totality reaction in which a thousand kinds of defensive readiness collaborate. In this process, interest in the survival of the whole seems to regulate the activity of many parts. Evidently all living things have the inherent goal of becoming a whole and of standing their ground in the struggle for existence.

Holism and Psychosomatics

It is obvious that body and soul are part of this totality as partial aspects of the *body-soul totality*. Any independent behavior of these two components will inevitably put a person on the wrong track. There never is one body *and* one soul; there only are the events of life which, depending on one's perspective, appear spiritual or physical. Anyone who says that there are psychological *causes* of physical illnesses makes a natural mistake. It is just as wrong to say that psychological disturbances are *caused* physically (perhaps by the autonomic nervous system or by unknown anomalies of the brain or the metabolism). It would be more correct to say that one and the same process has a more physical or a more psychological aspect, depending on the way one looks at it. Only on this viewpoint can a realistic *psychosomatic medicine* be based. A person does not have ulcers because of constant annoyance nor does he have high blood pressure because of constant readiness to fight or take flight. In the spirit of a holistic theory we must formulate the explanation this way: The ulcers and the annoyance, the hypertension and the anger (or timidity) are the expression of a unified life action which prevents the person from achieving communication with his fellowmen and hence overburdens the organism as an expressive organ. Where no linguistic community is achieved, the body speaks its "organ language," but we find the same isolation and destructiveness in the psychological realm as in the sick body.

If we have understood this view, we must also reconsider the theory of expression. In the psychology of the manners of expression there is an old dispute as to whether expression is to be regarded

as primarily biological and secondarily as psychological. Around the turn of the century James and
Lange formulated it this way: "We are sad because
we are crying!" In saying this they adopted the
viewpoint that certain physical processes primarily
constitute sadness; the psychological component
then is only an attendant phenomenon or epiphen-
omenon. Sound common sense, to be sure, would
be likely to take it the other way around: first one
is sad and then one cries. In the spirit of a holistic
theory of emotional life, however, we shall modify
the two theories and say that the subdued bodily
feeling and the sadness of the psyche are indistin-
guishably the same. Here, too, daily observation can
teach us many things. We are evidently dealing with
"circular" processes, of which one will try in vain
to find the beginning and the end. Thus high blood
pressure can apparently arise from being angry; on
the other hand, one gets angry much more easily if
one's blood pressure tends to be high. A body that
is weakened and lacks vitality will react to some
psychological frustration with a psychosomatic
depression much more quickly than a vigorously
functioning body. Hence any causal connection between the artificially isolated factors body and soul
is illusory.

In *psychopathology* and *characterology*, too,
we encounter totalities at every turn. As Adler always emphasized, every neurosis, for example, is
constructed like a "work of art"; its parts meaningfully fit the whole, the life-plan, the life-style, the
opinion which the individual in question has of
himself and the world. A person's character, too, is
never a mere collection of disparate habits, behavior
patterns, attitudes, and motivations. Any careful
character analysis demonstrates the blending of all
character traits into the unity of the personality.

There is no person in whose breast "two souls dwell." If one has pursued the investigation of a personality far enough, one will always see that all supposed inner and outer contradictions can be resolved; a person is a totality as far as his character is concerned too. With this insight the great writers of world literature have prepared the ground for psychology in inestimable fashion. While this scientific discipline was still trying to put man together like a mosaic of a thousand disconnected little stones, important writers were creating figures and personalities that seem true to life because psychologically they represent a totality.

Intuitive Perception of Wholeness

The idea of wholeness has long been supported by the art of biography as well. Every good biographer presents his hero subject in such a way that all parts of his personality are directed toward a totality. The life story of a person is not a chaotic jumble of events and outward strokes of fate. An individual certainly cannot foresee and predetermine his fate, but all facts of his life are more or less organized by the attitude with which they are accepted and processed. The biographer's art consists in illuminating for us the mentality of the protagonist through countless details of his actions or inaction. Often the personality of the politician, artist, scientist, philosopher, inventor, or other well-known person who is thus described is revealed through a tiny, random action which the biographer reports to us. Evidently the ability to see the totality of a life and to perceive it in all its details is a prerequisite for writing a good biography.

In this the biographer's art meets psychotherapy half-way; after all, the latter also constitutes biographical research. A psychoanalytic character analysis aims at investigating the nature of a person; at the end of a psychoanalytic treatment the analysand ought to know who he was, who he is, and who he can still become. To enable him to recognize this, multifarious clinical findings must be made and combined into a *synthetic picture*. The therapist or the therapeutic group joins the analysand in studying his present situation (with respect to such aspects as work, love, community, relationship to himself and to others, and attitudes), his case history (childhood, education, early childhood memories, economic and social conditions), and also his expectations and hopes for the future— and all this in light of the *unity of the personality*.

It is, to be sure, easier to speak of the wholeness of the person than to reconstruct it apperceptively. We are so accustomed to splitting psychological elements into individual functions that the detail to be analyzed makes us forget the whole. Modern psychological research in particular has followed an unfortunate guidepost in this respect. Because it patterned itself almost completely on the exact natural sciences, it concentrated, in their spirit, on analytic thought. The "atoms" of emotional life were fastened upon in hopes of gradually coming to grips with the complete psyche through psychological atomism. This, however, was only a dreamlike, distant goal; in reality these researchers continued to investigate tiny psychic details with a great display of pseudoexactness. Measuring, counting, weighing, and experimenting were uncritically transferred from physics and chemistry to psychology. Research findings did not carry weight until they could be processed statistically; this yielded accurately obtained trivia which were of no use and no concern to anyone. Psychology oriented toward the

Some Individual Functions Which Must Be Viewed Against the Background of the Total Personality

Perception	Thought	Feeling Moods
Volition	Drives (sexuality, hunger)	Imagination
Daydreams Nocturnal dreams	Memory	Attitudes Motivations Interests
Mimicry	Gestures	Postures Behavior
Habits	Handwriting Diction Clothing	Gait Life-style Opinion
Character (goals, outline, plans)	Early childhood memories	Symptomatic acts, psychic and psychosomatic symptoms
Ways of thinking Ideals Conscience	Intelligence	Talents Gifts
Consciousness	Unconscious	Value horizon
Prejudices	Political orientation	Religious or philosophical world view
Past	Present	Future

(Every part *determines* all other parts and is determined by them, but no one part is the cause of any other part.)

natural sciences, from Wilhelm Wundt to the present, has left us whole libraries of research material
which, for all practical purposes, turns out to be
more or less insignificant. Yet the isolating and experimental approach continues to be taught and
practiced at the universities, because these people
simply do not feel up to a psychology of the "whole
man" as he lives, acts, suffers, loves, searches for
meaning, breathes, and dies. Depth psychology,
however, stands and falls with this holistic concept,
which must be gained intuitively and can only be
experienced and properly understood in psychotherapeutic practice.

The table on the preceding page lists some psychological functions and their manifestations,
which will be clarified in the following pages in
terms of their reciprocal effects and significance for
the totality.

Part and Whole of the Psyche

A person's *perception* appears to be a relatively
independent function within the total emotional
life. With the aid of our sense organs we form an
image of the outside world as we think it really is.
This view is misleading, however; perception is
anything but an exact mirror of the conditions in the
world. Rather, any perception is greatly colored by
the total personality making it. Our picture of the
world around us is shaped by our feelings, drives,
emotions, moods, and even our fantasies. Hence the
perceptions of different people never coincide exactly. The German painter Ludwig Richter tells in
his memoirs that, together with two friends, he tried
to paint the same landscape near Rome as realisti-
cally as possible, but three completely different
landscapes resulted because each of the friends saw
the trees, shrubs, fields, and woods "through his

quite personal temperament." Thus one can say that perceptions can be an aid in the diagnosis of a personality, and they are so used by the so-called projective tests such as the Rorschach. What is perceived and how it is perceived are profoundly characteristic of a person's special nature, his interests, and his orientation toward life.

In academic psychology, *thought, feeling, and volition* have often been presented as isolated elements. Thus there has been an actual psychology of thought and a psychology of feeling and volition; in the case of the latter there have even been popular methods of specific "will training." This approach must be subjected to criticism as well. In every thought process emotional and voluntary admixtures play a considerable part. We reflect about a state of affairs or a problem more easily and more successfully if it arouses positive feelings in us. Our ability to solve a problem requires not only our thinking power but also our will power and our application generally, i.e., a readiness to muster good feelings for "obstacles of life." Even today this fact is frequently ignored in the so-called intelligence test, which measures the intelligence quotient as if there could be such a thing as an independent intelligence in a human being. The opposite is the case, however; all intelligence depends on a person's disposition (as indicated by his accessibility, his discrimination, his openness to social relationships, etc.) Many ostensibly stupid children with low measured IQs are not stupid at all but emotionally blocked. Their intelligence could be greatly improved if their total personality were raised to a higher level by processes of social maturation.

Anyone who has properly understood the totality approach will always avoid singling out some factor of emotional life and trying to postulate the

primary psychological force in it. In the psyche
everything is connected with everything else, and
nothing can be construed as the *primary cause*. This
mistake is made, for example, by orthodox psychoanalysis when it makes the sex drive (the libido) the
driving force of all emotional life. Thus the very
broadly conceived sexuality comes to be considered
the cause of feelings, thoughts, dreams, cultural
achievements, and nervous symptoms. Viewed holistically, sexual desire in all its forms certainly has
a great psychologically determinative capacity, but
it is nowhere a preferred causal element. For sexuality not only determines the feelings; the feelings
also determine sexuality. It is similar with thought,
volition, perception, sense of value, and imagination. The untrammeled generalizations of the
Freudians must today undergo multifarious correc-
tions in the light of holistic psychology. Thus, sexual
perversions, for example, can never be traced to an
infantile sexual imprint alone; only the emotional
fates of such patients (but also other factors such as
their religion and their *Weltanschauung*) make it
possible really to come to grips with their deformed
sexuality.

Does sexuality determine *imagination* or does
the imagination determine sexuality? Both questions are formulated too narrowly. A more refined
analysis will always show that our fantasizing is dependent on all the other psychic functions and also
acts upon them. There is nothing to justify short-
ening this chain of conditions or reducing the imagination to the sex drive, the power urge, or the self-
assertion drive. Since fantasizing often extends to
the future, one could debate whether as an outline
of the future it is dependent on a person's past. As
psychoanalytic therapy can easily demonstrate, this
surely is the case. On the other hand, however, a

person's memory also is permeated by elements of fantasy, i.e., we never remember the past the way it really was but the way our imagination constantly reshapes it. Hence everyone ought to call his memoirs *Dichtung und Wahrheit* (Poetry and Truth), as Goethe did. Our memory is an imaginative artist and transforms all the material it finds within it in accordance with its emotional condition and perspectives of the future. Thus the present situation of a person also influences what he projects into his future and his past; this is why at various stages of his life a person has completely different memories of his childhood and development as well as completely different fantasies about the future.

This approach can also be applied to the *interpretation of dreams* (as well as daydreams). It would be a mistake to characterize dreams as a mere reflex of childhood fate, as infantile sexual wishes, or as an expression of age-old human experience (the collective unconscious). Dreams contain emotional life in its totality—namely, our anxieties and apprehensions, our hopes and our desires, our character and our instincts, our reason and our emotionality. Hence any interpretation of dreams in terms of a single cause should be rejected out of hand. In fact, upon closer examination even the search for *causes* of the dream turns out to be shortsighted. A dream is a symbol of our attitude toward all the problems of our life; in it the dreamer's childhood, his present situation, and his orientation toward the future are seamlessly combined. A reduction of the dream content to the so-called wish fulfillment and the reflection of long past childhood dramas turns partial aspects of understanding into absolutes, although of course these aspects should not be neglected. Nor should a dream be turned into a mystical object of concern out of which a whole world of religious secrets can be conjured after it has been conjured into it theoretically (which is what happened in the Jung school).

All *expressive phenomena* (such as mimicry, gestures, posture, habits, handwriting, diction, clothing) are permeated by the "life style" (A. Adler) and the stylish unity of the personality. This enables the connoisseur of human nature to divine the character structure of a person from tiny details of expression. A great deal of practice, self-knowledge, and a genuine relationship with one's fellowmen are required for this. In psychotherapy it is of the greatest importance to note even the subtlest expressive actions and to use them for diagnosing the personality. The skill of the psychotherapist consists in letting the patient act upon him unconstrainedly, in absorbing him, as it were, benevolently and without anxiety, so that the psychotherapist can see with the patient's eyes, hear with his ears, and feel with his feelings. Genuine understanding can only grow out of this holistic identification, and only when the patient feels understood can he get well.

Traditional academic psychology was, among other things, *aptitude* research. It concerned itself with supposedly innate talents, abilities, and skills which were minutely investigated with particular attention to heredity. Thus, for example, family trees of brilliant and talented people were constructed. The general population thinks it understands some readiness for achievement if an uncle or a grandfather was able to accomplish something similar ("He's good at figures because Uncle Jonathan always was a prize pupil in arithmetic!"). Alfred Adler passionately fought this superstition about heredity. Basically, no person is able to ascertain what is truly inherited. In constructing fam-

ily trees (and also in the case of mental illness) people forget that there is always a *tradition* in families,
which means that upbringing alone produces much
similarity as far as talents, neuroses, psychoses, and
intelligence are concerned.

Then, too, the talent hypothesis is very fatalistic. It seems like an offshoot of religious thought:
no one can influence or predetermine the divine
"election." Depth psychology tends to trace a person's abilities to his training, his courage, his interest, and his possible identifications; man is a learning creature, and (almost) everything he can do he
has learned within the framework of cultural influences. For the rest, one must clearly realize that
talents are not isolated phenomena in emotional
life; they thrive only when a developed social interest, a wealth of feeling, a capacity for dedication,
patience, an ethos of the personality, enthusiasm,
and devotion to a cause are also present. Talent research limited to its special subject is of no use to
us; investigations of talent must always be anchored
in a psychology of personality.

Orthodox psychoanalysis introduced a division
of the human personality into the *conscious* and the
unconscious. In the late work of Freud we even find
the three psychic authorities ego, id, and superego,
all of which are treated as if they were independent
miniature persons; at any rate, the ego, the id, and
the superego can constantly struggle with one another and keep one another in check. Because of
this intrapsychic civil war, the totality of the person
is actually forgotten; if one reads the descriptions
of the psychoanalysts, one gets the impression that
the prevailing condition of the psyche is "war of
everyone against everyone." This hypothesis, too,
is based on inexact observations and hasty generalizations. After careful exploration one will always

find that in the conscious mind of a person are almost exactly the same attitudes and postures as in
his unconscious. The latter is not a collection of wild
drives opposed to the moral and modest conscious.
Every person has an unconscious that fits the conscious orientation of his life. Here, too, we can demonstrate the unity of the personality. Even in the
neuroses it is not the case that the patient consciously wants to be well and is only prevented from
being so by his unconscious. In his innermost being
every neurotic *knows* what he wants to achieve with
his symptoms (anxiety, depression, compulsive phenomena, "neurotic constitution," perversion), *why*
he has them, and what they do to *unburden* him in
the field of social relationships; he knows it, but he
does not *understand* (see through) it. Therapy must
illuminate this for him. In the process both the doctor and the patient recognize that one reaps in the
unconscious what one is in the habit of sowing in
the conscious. Anyone who constantly lives without
contact with his fellow human beings should not be
surprised if bad feelings, morbid instincts, and
aggressions are extracted from his unconscious.

According to Freud, the *conscience* is an aggressive instinct pushed inward. Aggressions which
because of educational and cultural influences cannot be abreacted outward turn inward and produce
the pangs of conscience from which civilized persons suffer. Accordingly a person faces the unpleasant choice of tormenting either himself or others; in
any case, he cannot escape torture. This is another
instance of nonholistic thinking, for there is nothing
that entitles us to trace complex phenomena of conscience solely to aggressive motivations. Certainly,
in depressive patients there are conscience reactions which strike one as rather autoaggressive, but
we must not disregard the fact that with his self-

accusations and threats of suicide a depressive person tortures not only himself but also those around him. Invariably his symptoms are also aimed at dominance over others who are depressed and perhaps even exploited by his malady.

Conscience depends not only on aggression but also on such factors as a person's thoughts, feelings, desires, fantasies, hopes, loves, and hates. It again is a symbol and emblem of the total personality. "Tell me what conscience you have, and I shall tell you what kind of person you are!"

In conclusion we should point out that in every respect there are holistic relationships between both a person's *character* and his *Weltanschauung*. A person's *Weltanschauung* arises from the depths of his emotional structure and always reacts upon it. The way a person thinks and feels about politics, religion, philosophy, and life can and should always be utilized for the diagnosis of his personality. In psychotherapy in particular, the *Weltanschauung* of a patient must always be included in the analysis. Often a neurosis is especially anchored in a person's philosophy of life (e.g., his religion or his political persuasion). Thus the neurosis cannot be cured if the patient's *Weltanschauung* is not corrected as well. A person's character is not manifested only in his social relationships; it is also contained in the prejudices and convictions of a person, and these can be very neurotic.

Predecessors of Holistic Thinking

Our attention having been drawn so emphatically to the *holistic theory of emotional life*, we must deal with the question of the origin of this conception and its originators. Reflections in the area of intellectual history give us reason to view it as an

ancient heirloom of cultural history whose origins
go back to the ancient Greeks. In modern times it
has been primarily philosophy that offered a home
to holistic thought. Medicine, too, has had a holistic
orientation at times, especially in the Romantic period; when it became oriented toward the natural
sciences, however, it increasingly adopted an isolating approach and abandoned the viewpoint of
wholeness in favor of an accurate analysis of parts.
Among the philosophers of the past who may be
regarded as pioneers of the holistic theory, Schopenhauer, Nietzsche, and Dilthey have pride of
place; modern depth psychology owes them an incalculable debt of gratitude.

Arthur Schopenhauer (1788–1860) is an ances-
tor of psychoanalysis, and Freud repeatedly referred to him appreciatively, though he admitted
that he did not become acquainted with the philosopher's works until a very late date. Schopenhauer's
thought constitutes a turning point in European philosophy. Until his advent almost all philosophers
were prejudiced in favor of reason, which they glo-
rified as the highest authority in human emotional
life, describing it as a divine or natural light in man.
Schopenhauer was one of the first who characterized reason as a plaything of affective, emotional,
and instinctual forces in human beings. To him reason is subordinate to the so-called will, by which
he means the totality of irrational psychological
forces, particularly drives and affects. The will is the
blind giant and reason the sighted dwarf whom the
former carries on his shoulders; the unreasonable
giant seldom goes where his knowing guide would
like to lead him. Many human actions are understandable only if one includes the dark background
of our emotional life as a motivational factor; our
rationality often serves to veil and cloak our irra-

tional driving forces. By referring to the affective determination of the processes of our thought and life Schopenhauer blazed the trail for a psychological and philosophical holistic theory.

Thus he was one of the first who knew how to unravel the meaning of dreams. Until that time dreams had been regarded as a "hint of the gods," as senseless happenings, as signs and wonders. In his main work, *Die Welt als Wille und Vorstellung*, 1819 [transl., *The World as Will and Idea*], Schopenhauer presents a realistic dream theory. The analogy by which he clarifies the origin of dreams has become famous. He says, among other things, that our life resembles a book that we can leaf through in approximate order, that is, page by page, while we are awake. It is different in a dream; there we leaf through it very capriciously, skipping entire pages and chapters, and this is why dreams seem so chaotic and senseless (although they never are). For all parts of a dream come from our book of life and thus are components of our lived life that can always be understood if we can find the context in which they belong. We have to fill in the gaps, as it were, which the dream in its incoherence keeps creating; then we shall comprehend what a dream tells us about ourselves and our position in life. If one reads the pertinent pages in Schopenhauer, one almost thinks that one is holding Sigmund Freud's *Interpretation of Dreams* in one's hands.

Schopenhauer also provides an outstanding theory of psychosis. For him a delusion is not a brain disease, nor is it a curse of God. In patients suffering from a delusion he notices that they monomaniacally cling to some notions that cannot be corrected. This rigidity of thought must be viewed with reference to corresponding "will processes" (that is, emotional reactions). What is it that causes the will

(the core of the personality) to be fixated so stub-
bornly on certain thought contents? Schopenhauer
already sees the patient's life history as the moti-
vation for the delusion formation. In his estimation,
this involves destinies that are in some form unbearable for the individual. The "will" refuses to
recognize certain realities because they are too
painful, too degrading, or too discouraging for it. As
the will rejects (*represses*, as we have been saying
since Freud) a bit of reality, a gap arises in the emotional life. This cannot be, and with the same energy
with which one tries to "get something out of one's
mind" one has to imagine something else, that is,
to hallucinate it. Processes of compensation play a
considerable part in this. One can cure the delusion
only if one finds the place where the retreat from
social reality began. One must also fill in the emotional gap which underlies the mental confusion.
Only then can the patient abandon his delusional
ideas, because he will then be able to restore the
wholeness of his personality.

With all these theses Schopenhauer discovered
the unconscious and sensitively analyzed it eighty
years before Freud. He is, incidentally, also the dis-
coverer of the enormous significance of sexuality for
all of emotional life. If one reads his treatise on "Me-
taphysik der Geschlechtsliebe" [Metaphysics of
sexual love] (in *Die Welt als Wille und Vorstellung*,
vol. 2), one can hardly add anything if one is a
Freudian. Schopenhauer also points out that the
course of a person's life appears as a peculiar totality. Anyone who views his life in retrospect will
recognize that everything clarifies a secret plan
which is hidden within ourselves. If one disregards
Schopenhauer's mysticism in this hypothesis, one
already finds here Adler's concept of the "life style"

which coherently shapes the course of a person's life.

Another achievement of Schopenhauer is that he was one of the pioneers of the so-called criticism of ideology. As we know, this strives to trace intellectual and cultural achievements to conditions outside thought, i.e., to relate false reasoning in particular to biological, social, psychic, economic, and political realities. Schopenhauer concerned himself with the fact that so many philosophers are unable to recognize truth and thus even propagate palpable errors and disseminate obvious falsehoods. This, too, must be understood in holistic terms. What dispositions of the will falsify the search for truth? In his contemporary fellow philosophers Schopenhauer recognizes above all their dependence on the state, the church, and public opinion as a truth-impeding factor. Anyone who by virtue of his mental attitude belongs to the masses, anyone whose occupation makes him dependent on a government or a church authority (and thus on his breadbasket) will always find in his search for truth only things that do not unduly jeopardize his position in life. Schopenhauer said that such thinkers have more *Absichten* (intentions) than *Einsichten* (insights). And this holds true for everyone; our cognition never extends beyond our courage (and our inner and outer independence). With these teachings Schopenhauer disseminated a salutary skepticism regarding all prevalent religious convictions behind which one usually finds power interests and hidden power politics. One has to be able to see this if one embarks on the difficult search for truth.

Friedrich Nietzsche (1844–1900) was a direct continuator of Schopenhauer's thought. He magnificently refined and developed the psychological

and philosophical criticism of ideology. Nietzsche
was exceedingly perceptive regarding the psychology of intellectual and cultural valuations. Needless
to say, he too was an outstanding representative of
holistic thought.

We owe to Nietzsche, whom both Freud and
Adler acknowledged as the progenitor of depth psychology, a psychology of morals, of religion, of philosophy, of culture generally. Entire volumes could
be written about the psychological achievements
that originated with him; we have to content ourselves with some brief references. Nietzsche was
excellent at deducing from intellectual phenomena
their total psychological and especially biological
context. In this respect his life work is a treasure
trove of holistic psychology. For example, he
analyzes the Christian religion as an uprising of
the slaves in the ancient world. The slaves (and
the Jews as well) smarted under the social and
political discrimination of the time. They were surrounded by Roman aristocrats whose lives were
governed by the exertion of power, by pleasure, and
by the untrammeled expansion of existence. Since
the slaves could not risk a direct uprising, they re-
volted in emotional, roundabout ways: they condemned all worldly orientation in thought and life,
spoiled pleasure and *joie de vivre*, and reached beyond the earth into an imaginary heaven in order to
devalue reality. Nietzsche calls this process *ressen-
timent*, a source of morality and religion. Here an
oppressed class of people secretly takes revenge on
its oppressors; it damns a world in which it cannot
rule, win, and expand. This is the derivation of the
Christian contempt for the world and the body, a
contempt that determined two thousand years of
European destiny. Nietzsche said: "From an ideal
I draw conclusions about those who need it!" Re-

ligion and its morality mark the ascendance to power of a pitiful type of person who has to diminish and degrade life in order to remain in power. Such analyses may be found in Nietzsche's work in great profusion; they constitute a barely exploited fund of knowledge which future investigators will have to elaborate on. The "Theory of the Will to Power" was an excellent key to depth psychological exploration; even in Adler's major work, *Über den nervösen Charakter* [*The Neurotic Constitution*], published in 1912, it is easy to feel Nietzsche's influence everywhere.

Wilhelm Dilthey (1833–1911) was the third precursor of the philosophical holistic theory. Here we think in particular of his famous treatise *Über eine beschreibende und zergliedernde Psychologie* [*On a Descriptive and Analytic Psychology*, 1894]. Dilthey, to be sure, was a great inspirer in a great many areas of intellectual life. The stimulation which the science of psychology received from him is only part of his comprehensive teaching and activity.

Dilthey was profoundly impressed by the fact that the psychology of his time was basically mechanistic and remote from life. In those days the so-called faculty psychology still held untrammeled sway; it divided emotional life into individual *faculties* (for example, the reasoning faculty) and described these in isolation. This abstract "natural scientific psychology" was in glaring contrast to the psychology that Dilthey found in the works of important writers. When Shakespeare, Goethe, Dostoievsky, Tolstoy, and others describe a person, we can see him or her standing before us; all parts correspond with the whole and are an expression and a symptom of the totality. Academic psychology makes grandiose claims of accuracy, but it describes only phantoms and not people of flesh and blood.

Dilthey now called for a psychology that would turn the intuitive knowledge of artists to account, that would be as true to life as literature and yet be scientific. To this end it would have to be descriptive and analytical; its first task would be an extensive description of psychological experiences and its second task the showing of psychological *structures*, i.e., purpose-structured totalities which constitute the psychological reality.

According to Dilthey, everything psychological is structurally organized; it must be viewed and understood in holistic terms. This includes a rejection of the intellectual attitude of natural science. Dilthey is a champion of a humanistic psychology that attempts to follow the methodological model of the humanities (including history, philology, art history, and philosophy). The basic concepts of such psychological research include totality, structure, meaning, significance, context of life, goal and purpose, self-realization, and value realization. Dilthey not only inaugurated this kind of psychology but also strove to apply it to the phenomena of cultural and intellectual life, particularly to the modes in which individuality appears in practical life and in the formation of culture. As a pupil of the great philosopher Dilthey, Eduard Spranger took up and developed many of his suggestions. Spranger's *Lebensformen* [Forms of life], published in 1922, made a contribution to philosophical anthropology and hence also to basic psychological research. The *understanding* of purpose connections is put on an equal footing with the *explaining* of causal connections, the understandable structures being regarded as more essential. Explainable facts and consequences are not real life processes but synthetic products of "denatured" life.

From Dilthey the path of modern psychology leads via Edmund Husserl and Martin Heidegger to Jean Paul Sartre, who produced a profound elaboration of the holistic idea in his phenomenological existentialism. This orientation is shared by the so-called existential analysis of L. Binswanger and M. Boss, in whose presentations psychic elements are always viewed and interpreted holistically.

We now leave philosophy and turn to the question of what impulses in psychology provide the basis of modern holistic theory. What comes to mind first is the *gestalt* theory, which constitutes a decisive break with psychological atomism and mechanism. In 1890 Christian von Ehrenfels introduced the concept *gestalt quality* (founded content) into psychology. On the basis of optical figures and melodies he was able to demonstrate that perception is not composed of atomistic particles; we see or hear entire configurations which have the characteristics of *superabundance* and *transposability* (a melody can be transposed into various keys, and while the notes are different, the melody remains the same). This meant that elementarism (or content psychology) and associationism (or associative psychology), for which Wilhelm Wundt had secured preeminent status at the universities since 1874, were modified in one important respect: the holistic tendencies of emotional life could now no longer be ignored, although the gestalt theory at first limited itself to the psychology of perception.

Hans Cornelius (Munich) was soon able to demonstrate, however, that the emotions also have gestalt quality. Felix Krüger (Leipzig), later Wundt's successor, supplemented these findings with the holistic hypothesis, which he first introduced under the term *Komplexqualität* (unstructured qualities).

Krüger then evolved a true holistic psychology, which in the course of time gave rise to a whole school.

The theoreticians of gestalt psychology (Köhler, Koffka, Wertheimer, Metzger, Lewin, and others) demonstrated in their very interesting writings to what a great extent a person is constantly forming configurations in his perception, thoughts, feelings, desires, fantasies, and actions. Consciousness is not passive like a camera or a reflex machine; always and everywhere it seeks to actualize meaningful configurations in space, time, and movement. Good configurations are realized if the psychosomatic organism is up to par; if, however, it is damaged in any way, then a deterioration takes place spasmodically rather than continually. What is then aimed for are more primitive configurations, which require less expenditure of energy, agility, and understanding. Kurt Goldstein applied this insight very fruitfully to the investigation of brain injuries and their aftereffects; our understanding of aphasia was also considerably enhanced by such considerations. The development of gestalt theory paralleled that of depth psychology, and at first there seems to have been little mutual influence. Only Kurt Lewin was able to build many bridges between the two disciplines during his research in the United States. Today we see the beginnings of new syntheses between these related doctrines.

Our discussion proceeded from the fact that in his individual psychology Alfred Adler gave most incisive expression to holistic theory within the framework of depth psychology. Particularly in his therapeutic practice he constantly emphasized the need to adopt a holistic viewpoint. Adler taught his pupils to weave all details of a personality together artistically and to perceive the whole in every detail. Thus, in a therapy based on individual psychology, any work disturbance will first be connected with a person's love life and sex life, which the therapist will try to understand on the basis of the patient's attitude toward him and his behavior during counseling. The next step is the patient's image of himself and others, which the therapist will explain on the basis of the patient's social relationships in early childhood; his first childhood memories will be interpreted in light of the present complications and behavioral difficulties. All the above-mentioned items may clearly illuminate the dreams presented by the analysand, which may provide a key to preferred characterological attitudes, and such attitudes always interact with ideological positions, religion, and political and other attitudes.

It is evident that a psychotherapist has to set in motion a *circular process of cognition.* He must never finish prematurely; any quick determination and generalization should be proscribed in this delicate work of understanding. It takes someone with great inner maturity and personal clearheadedness to keep his attention free-floating for as long as possible and not to stop at half-truths or quarter-truths. The apperceptive organ which the psychologist or therapist uses here is nothing less than his personality. If this instrument is stunted or handicapped, his apperception will be correspondingly diminished. Only someone who consciously feels himself to be a totality can perceive holistic elements in other people in fairly undistorted form. People with sparse emotional equipment will hardly ever be successful as psychotherapists. They will judge their patients by the criteria of their own meagerness and thus impede rather than promote their patients' further development. In psychoanalysis, too, it is not possible to give one's analysands more than one possesses.

In Alfred Adler's work we find so many statements expressing a holistic viewpoint that we could cite these passages ad infinitum. We shall present in conclusion only one passage from the writings of the great psychologist and therapist which logically connects totality with the fact that a person fashions his own character, his own personality, and his own life-style as an artist fashions a work of art. It is self-evident that one approaches a work of art with a claim to wholeness and will not divide it into disparate parts for the purpose of "explaining" it. Because Adler was motivated by the feeling that every person is a unique and unmistakable work of art, he wrote in his book *The Education of Children* (London 1957; Allen & Unwin):

The unity of the personality is inherent in the existence of every human being. Every individual represents in equal measure the unity and wholeness of the personality and the individual shaping of this unity. Thus an individual is both picture and artist. He is the artist of his own personality. But as an artist he is neither a perfect craftsman nor a person with infallible understanding of his soul and his body. Rather, an individual is an extremely fallible and imperfect being.

In viewing the personality structure, we notice as the main structural defect that its wholeness, its particular goal in life, and the life style peculiar to it are not founded on objective reality but on the individual's subjective view of the facts of life. The conceptual idea, the comprehension of a fact, is never the fact itself. For this very reason all persons living in the same factual world assume different forms. Every person forms himself in accordance with his personal conception of things, and some conceptions are psychically healthier than others. In the development of a person we must always reckon with such individual errors and disturbances. Above all, we must take into account the misinterpretations of early child-hood, for they exert an essential influence on the further course of our life.

4

Ways of Exploring the Human Personality

Knowledge of Human Nature as Science

One way in which individual psychology's closeness to life manifests itself is that it furnishes a basis for a practical knowledge of human nature more than do all other psychological schools. It was Adler's intent to make knowledge of human nature teachable. What had for thousands of years been the random gift of individuals was to become common property through teaching and training. The intuitive understanding of the emotional stirrings of one's fellowmen which poets, actors, pedagogues, and businessmen occasionally acquired can hardly be transmitted to posterity; only when an understanding of human nature is cast in scientific rules can it become a secure tradition in which coming generations can profit from the experience of their predecessors.

Adler viewed his work as a continuation of the achievements of the great psychologists of all times, especially the achievements of popular wisdom and of literature; in this regard he singled out the works of Homer, Goethe, Dostoievsky, and others. For him psychopathology became the point of departure for a deeper understanding of the normal psyche as well. The practical aspect of treating people, which is decisive in depth psychology, was to be given pride of place in everyday life as well. Again and again Adler pointed out that errors in the under- standing of human nature cause not only material damage but frequently also unspeakable suffering and entanglements. An individual seldom clearly realizes where he has failed in his understanding of a fellowman, and even when faulty judgment has catastrophic consequences, there still is no guar- antee that the harmed person will recognize the true sources of error in his judgment.

The consequences of this lack of understanding of human nature are devastating for both the indi- vidual and the community at large. Adler points out to what a great extent people live, talk, and think past one another. Not only is a false estimate of spouses, children, and parents an everyday occur- rence within a family, but political and social life is also impaired because people know too little about themselves and their fellowmen. Political catas- trophes (demagoguery, dictatorship, the rule of fa- natics, the rampancy of prejudiced thought and col- lective aggression) are often due to the fact that people are not able to see through their rulers and fall victim to the promises of loquacious psycho- paths and hypocritical purveyors of political blar- ney. Mankind is slow to learn from its mistakes and keeps falling prey to the promises and blandish- ments of its power-hungry leaders, whose deficient social interest behind their ringing phrases could easily be unmasked by a more profound understand- ing of human nature.

Although Adler's understanding of human na- ture is formulated in scientific terms, it also has sig- nificant artistic aspects. This is clearly revealed in the demand that the personality be grasped as a unity, with an empathy similar to that with which an artist grasps his object before depicting it. Un-

derstanding a person thus does not mean a mechanical stringing together of individual test data,
but a divination of his law of movement and his style
of life—a putting of oneself in his place, as it were.
The scientific apparatus is a mere aid, a signpost
on an arduous road. A judge of human nature should
be so familiar with it that in the face of the fellow
human being he is striving to understand he is able
to forget it in order to get a better perception of the
uniqueness of his personality.

The most reliable results in the evaluation of a
person derive from the interpretation of an entire
course of a life that is interpreted on the basis of
individual psychology. If one knows a person's
childhood situation and compares it with the reactions of the adult, one can draw a line of movement
that is astonishingly constant. The longitudinal section of a human life also permits one to draw conclusions about the future of the subject; once one
has familiarized oneself with a person's guideline,
it is possible to predict how he will behave in one
situation or another. This kind of knowledge permits insights into the human conduct of life that are
more far-reaching than anything that was taught
under this rubric prior to depth psychology. Beyond
that it also makes it possible for us to escape the
compulsion of unconscious stereotypes and to help
us and others transcend acquired weaknesses.

Adler's desire to teach how to understand
human nature stemmed from his awareness of the
deleterious consequences of a deficiency in this regard. To him the general isolation of one person
from another, mutual misunderstandings in love
and marriage, and the chaotic condition of our social
life were consequences of our ignorance of our fellow human beings. Even our education fills us with
a thousand prejudices which we carry from child-

hood to adulthood without examining them. The one-sidedness of our experiences compels us to adopt standpoints that are detrimental to an understanding of larger connections. Hence the knowledge of human nature among human beings is in the same situation as chemistry was in when it still was alchemy.

According to Adler, the best judges of human nature will be those who have kept up active contacts with their fellow human beings and with life generally. Those who have experienced both the heights and depths of human life, possibly through their own fault, and who have had the strength to change their ways (in other words, the "repentant sinners") also have a chance to understand more and better than the self-righteous and the philistines. First and foremost, however, those will be rewarded with a fuller knowledge of their fellow human beings who have been taught by their greater social interest to share in the troubles of others. Any training in human understanding that proposes to be not mere theory but practice must culminate in this. To Adler it was primarily an instrument for human mutual aid, and thus he could justifiably postulate it as a science "which is practiced hardly anywhere else but which seems to us to be the most important occupation and one that is indispensable for all strata of the population."

First Childhood Recollections

One of Adler's important discoveries concerns the interpretability of the earliest childhood recollections. In his *Psychopathology of Everyday Life*, Freud had already drawn attention to the so-called cover memories. In this he utilized the earliest memories of his patients in line with his theory of repression, assuming that the memory constitutes a falsification and modification of repressed experiences. Adler's teachings about early childhood recollections proceed from entirely different premises, which are based on his theory of memory.

Memory and recollections are not simply a depot of impressions and sensations but components of purposeful emotional life. Perception itself is not simply a neutral photographic plate on which environmental objects and events are depicted; on the contrary, what a person perceives is characteristic of him and indicates his orientation and the direction of his interest. Memory, too, constitutes a psychic act of processing. Its material is subject to a process of selection and sifting, and according to Adler, only that remains fresh and reproducible which appears usable for an individual's position toward life. Hence a person's memories are extremely revealing of his nature, since from a wealth of impressions those things are selected that provide an impetus or a deterrent but in any case a confirmation of the chosen style of life. Memory digests its experiences; it transforms them, as it were, and assimilates them only when it has adapted the disparate impressions to the total personality. Accordingly, in Adler's view it is diagnostically very valuable to know the first childhood memories of a person, be they real or fantasized. From them the expert who knows how to analyze their affective tone and opinion content can derive the life program of the person concerned. For memory always contains a plan for the future—only a person's store of memories enables him to provide for his future, and what will remain in his memory is what he consciously or unconsciously regards as essential for his future.

From such memory fragments the psychologist and judge of human nature can learn a great deal about a person's character and his attitude toward life. There are no hard and fast rules or ruses here, of course. Only on the basis of a profound and trained psychological understanding can one use such psychic details as a reference to the underlying total picture. Let us quote Adler himself on the basic points of this procedure:

Provided, of course, that we use the utmost care and possess the greatest experience, we are now in a position to discover, mostly from the earliest recollections, the mistaken direction of the life path as well as the lack of social interest or its opposite. In this we are particularly guided by our knowledge of a lack of social interest, of its causes and consequences. Much comes to light through the presentation of a We or I situation or through the mention of the mother. Accounts of dangers and accidents as well as of corporal and other punishments reveal the exaggerated inclination to keep in mind particularly the hostile side of life. The recollection of the birth of a sibling discloses the situation of dethronement; the recollection of the first visit to the kindergarten or school shows the great impression produced by new situations. The memory of sickness and death often is linked with a fear of these dangers and frequently with an attempt to be better equipped to meet them, perhaps as a doctor, a nurse, or in similar fashion. Recollections of a stay in the country with the mother, as well as the mention of certain persons such as the mother, the father, or the grandparents in a friendly atmosphere often show not only a preference for these persons, who evidently pampered the child, but also the exclusion of others. Recollections of misdeeds, thefts, and sexual activities usually indicate a great effort to exclude these from future experience. Occasionally one learns also of other inclinations, such as visual, auditory, or motor interests, which may give occasion to uncover failures in school as well as a mistaken occupational choice and may enable one to suggest an occupation that is in keeping with a better preparation for life.

(*Der Sinn des Lebens*, pp. 138–39)

In this connection it is tempting to interpret one of the earliest childhood recollections of Adler himself. The thesis that one's first memories express one's life-style can easily be confirmed, since according to Adler "there is no such thing as innocuous memories." Thus he tells in one of his works that as a child he had to walk through a cemetery on his way to school:

I was frightened every time, and with great displeasure I watched other children walk through the cemetery unconcernedly while I took step after step full of anxiety and dread. Apart from the unbearable fear, I was tormented by the thought that I was less brave than the others. One day I made up my mind to put a stop to this mortal dread, and as a means to this end I again chose induration. I remained a stretch behind the other children, put my satchel on the ground near the cemetery wall, and ran across the cemetery about a dozen times until I felt I had mastered my fear. I believe that from that time on I passed along this path without fear.

The interpretation of this recollection also includes this instructive addition: Adler was able to find out that there was no cemetery on his way to school. Thus the entire occurrence is fictitious, a fantasy, albeit one that is profoundly characteristic of the contriver. One recognizes from it a courageous type of person who trains himself to overcome his fear of life. His desire not to take a back seat to others leads him to make resolute efforts. His recollection also teaches us that he optimistically believes in his success and always keeps in mind that all anxieties can be mastered through resoluteness.

Individual Psychology and Testing Methods

Adler warned against placing the widely used tests at the center of the diagnosis of the personality. He advised his pupils to avoid these shortcuts and to develop their intuition. The latter is best employed in a psychotherapeutic dialogue without any presuppositions. The artificial situation of a test can only supply ambiguous results, and this situation is not changed by the mathematically exact evaluation of which the testing specialists are so proud. In that way homage is paid to an idol of psychological measurement whose results are of little value for depth psychology.

A test is a spot check, and originally tests were little spot checks by means of which an attempt was made to measure certain human abilities and capabilities. Commerce and industry started using such techniques decades ago when they set about, sometimes in line with the scientific management of the American Frederick Winslow Taylor, to specialize working procedures to a very great extent and to select for a highly mechanized activity "the best man in the best place." Since the economy of that time (and unfortunately to a great extent today's economy as well) had little interest in the whole person, since a working person was regarded as a kind of tool, there seemed to be some justification for developing testing methods for such tools. So-called psychotechnics took up this demand on a large scale and people began to test in all kinds of situations. The numerical evaluation and the formalism of the method seemed to guarantee that an "objective" judgment could be made about a person's worth and aptitude.

Like industrial psychology, psychiatry at an early age developed testing methods that aimed at a differentiation between the psychological and intellectual abilities of normal and abnormal persons. In some respects psychiatry and the profit-oriented business world followed the same atomistic approach. Deriving from the same era, the psychiatric tests also viewed a person as a motley cluster of individual functions, such as intelligence, memory, feeling, and affect, which, with the proper methodology, ought to be measurable, countable, and weighable.

Individual psychology certainly does not reject the psychiatric testing methods *in toto*. Some techniques are not without usefulness if one wishes to test memory and intelligence. The use of normative and standardized test questions most easily permits comparisons which, if interpreted very cautiously, make possible a certain evaluation of the person tested. The awkward thing about even such unpretentious tests, however, is their isolation of the psychological functions. This is based on the assumption that in emotional life intelligence is neatly separated from other abilities, and yet even a layman knows that intelligence, feeling, and affect are mutually dependent. The gravest reproach which individual psychology levels against almost all testing methods refers to the fact that hardly any tests provide "dynamic findings"; they tell us nothing about the psychological tendencies or inhibitions that produce one reaction or another, about whether we are dealing with something changeable or unchangeable, or about what steps might be taken to effect an improvement or advancement. In practice one frequently finds that test results are misused to label persons. For example, children whose failure in school evidently has as its true cause emotional suffering because of an unhappy situation at home or in school are, on the basis of a test, designated as "untalented" or "unintelligent," with all the consequences for their future which derive from this.

If a great and dangerous responsibility is inherent in the testing of individual psychological functions, the matter becomes still more weighty when the total evaluation of a personality—for example, whether it is sound or sick, and the kind and degree of abnormality—is involved. Here, too, tests have come into general use in the last decades about which individual psychology has the greatest reservations.

Thus the Rorschach test is commonly applied. Hermann Rorschach, a Swiss psychiatrist, published his *Formdeutversuch* in 1920. It is a series of ink blots, accidental forms which the examinee is supposed to interpret just as he sees fit. His statements are taken down exactly and then subjected to a very detailed evaluative process. According to the theory, both symptoms and definite personality traits are expressed in very specific test results, so that the test can be used to measure the intelligence, the affectivity, the inner resources, and the classification of the personality. It is evidently a fact that health and illness pervade all modes of behavior of a person and that his nature can express itself in everything he does or does not do. Why, then, should it not manifest itself in a test result as well? But here, too, the greatest caution is indicated. The mechanical procedure of a test and its schematizing evaluation often disregard the uniqueness and inimitability of the personality. Of course, the reason why such methods and ploys are popular is that even the humanly paltriest "expert" carries around his yardstick, with which he thinks he can make an exact measurement of all people. Thus the testing methods always involve the risk that there will not be any human encounter with the person tested.

After all, no such encounter is necessary; the person will be counted and measured, the scheme functions like clockwork, and the precious instrument of empathy and understanding atrophies because it is replaced by the "machinery."

Thus individual psychology is very critical toward *all* testing methods, including such banal and sometimes absurd processes as the Szondi Test, the Thematic Apperception Test, and the tree-drawing test which have come into use. In accordance with Adler's advice and practice it utilizes for psychological diagnosis the *expressive movements* of the patient or the person seeking counseling, for example his facial expression, gestures, behavior, speech, gait, voice, gaze, but it never creates artificial test situations, which are bound to falsify the results. The decisive diagnosis, however, is always derived from the *life history*, which to a connoisseur unmistakably reveals a person's pace and life-style. Furthermore, a person's behavior in psychotherapy is itself a valuable diagnostic aid that is indispensable to a good observer for the evaluation of what the patient reports from his life and thought.

At a time when testing methods seem to be swamping everything, individual psychology teaches us to focus on the simplest means of understanding the psyche and to reject artificial processes in favor of direct contact, as well as an understanding and helpful human dialogue.

Individual Psychology and the Interpretation of Dreams

Adler's contributions in this field are based on Freud's epoch-making book *The Interpretation of Dreams* (1900), but they sharply differ from the theories of orthodox psychoanalysis. To Adler a dream is not wish fulfillment in the spirit of infantile sexuality. Dreams are not simply a revival of the dreamer's past as a child. They may have a regressive aspect here or there, but their nature is a psychic progression, that is, the dreamer's coming to terms with the problems of his life. Even in his sleep a person has a connection with the social tasks of life. Freud divined some of these things, but because of his narrow theoretical system he interpreted more from dreams than may actually be found there.

The role of dream interpretation is different in individual psychology from what it is in the other psychological schools. It is neither the "royal road to the unconscious" (Freud) nor an expression of the "collective unconscious" (Jung), but only a secondary component of psychotherapy. For various reasons, individual psychology regards the procedures of the many therapists who over the years collect thousands of dreams as quite inappropriate. In the final analysis, this derives from the specific goals of the psychotherapy of individual psychology. Adler considered it his task to give a neurotic person, whose orientation toward life and social interest had been damaged by unfavorable childhood experiences, needed courage and insight into his problems through cooperative conversations. This made him adopt an *active stance* in the psychotherapeutic realm. As a consequence, the *free association* of psychoanalysis was replaced by *purposive conversation*. At the same time the open-ended interpretation of dreams was abandoned, for Adler was of the opinion that a dream during sleep *essentially shows nothing else than a person's thinking, feeling, acting, and fantasizing during his wakeful state.*

According to Adler's teaching, a person's entire psychic activity is oriented toward coming to terms with the eternally pressing problems and questions of life. The way in which a person copes with his situation is always predetermined by his experiences in early childhood; this is done within the framework of the life-style acquired early on, in which all suitable and unsuitable reactions for the protection of the personality can be developed. Since all tasks of an individual's life derive from his fellowmen around him, every manifestation of life is in the nature of a *position* toward his own existence and his environment. This position will be shaped primarily by a person's self-esteem and the degree of his sense of solidarity with his fellowmen, and it must always satisfy his endeavor "to get from a minus situation to a plus situation." Fantasizing is subject to this existential law as well. Daydreams, for example, contain for the most part unmistakably fantasy-oriented and wish-oriented feelings, and these frequently appear in situations of insufficiency and frustration, with the typical tendency to raise the daydreamer's self-esteem in compensatory fashion.

Like daydreams, nocturnal dreams also deal with the life of the dreamer. Freud had proceeded from the assumption that every dream contains a "day's residue," some point of contact with the experiences of the day *before* the dream, which in roundabout ways endowed deeper childhood wishes with the energy to penetrate from the unconscious to the "preconscious." Adler (and at about the same time Alfonse Mäder) countered this theory based on the dreamer's past with a *prospective* dream theory, according to which the dream deals not so much with the past as with the future of the dreamer. The basic tendency of the psyche to be directed at the anticipation of coming tasks and dangers also applies to the psychic activity of the sleeper. After all, at bottom the sleeper is the same person as the waking person; he has the same thoughts and feelings, and although his perceptual activity is diminished, he is nevertheless more or less connected with his surroundings. It is in this sense that the dream, according to Adler, deals with the *life situations in store for the dreamer.*

The sleeping state determines the special nature of the dream presentation. Imagistic, purely associative thinking comes to the fore, and logic and sound common sense are replaced by a more affective view with a markedly subjective coloration. Since every psychological manifestation has a meaning and a purpose, the question as to the reason is decisive in the case of dreams as well. According to Adler, the dreamer dreams in order to ascertain his attitude toward life in the face of a pressing problem—to start his calculation of a future behavior, as it were, to initiate his movement aiming at the safeguarding of his personality. It does not matter whether he remembers his dream or forgets most of it. It is enough if the dream leaves traces of mood and feeling which daytime thought and action can utilize, guided by the person's unconscious philosophy of life, which is concretized in innumerable automatic reactions, character traits, opinions, convictions, and the like. It is up to the interpreter to fashion a dream totality out of the preserved dream fragments (which Freud called the *manifest* dream) by interpreting, amplifying, construing, etc. with the aid of the dreamer. Adler regarded such a search for the "latent dream" as unnecessary and confined himself to establishing a connection, insofar as possible, with the daily behavior and the particular situation facing the dreamer. In this sense a dream was for him only an incidental illustration for *character analysis*, that is, the analysis of living conduct which is to give the patient an understanding of himself and of the difficulties of his life.

Individual psychology does not necessarily see a dream as a slice of resuscitated childhood life, and it is cautious enough to project into dreams neither the Oedipus complex nor "unconscious religious needs." All it looks for in dreams is the *line of movement* through which a person seeks to overcome his conflicts. Here it contents itself with making an approximate estimate of the emotional content, the basic thoughts, and the "driving movement" of the dream (such as retreat, fear, forward striving, movement toward or away from people), being well aware that the conduct of the dreamer furnishes the final and decisive commentary on his dream. "The purpose of the interpretation of dreams that is practiced by us is to show the patient [and the dreamer in general] his preparations, which usually unmask him as the arranger of his suffering, to demonstrate to him how, leaning on parables and episodes, he seeks to grasp actual problems in a way that will permit him the exertion of his individual . . . striving."

Individual psychology displays the same cautious attitude in questions of *dream symbolism.* Adler accepted symbolic interpretations within certain limits, but he warned against translating every incomprehensible dream content into the technical language of a special theory. In particular, the attempt "to declare uncomprehended elements in a dream to be sexual symbols and then to find that everything stems from the libido" seemed completely wrongheaded to him. An interpretation of dreams without a thorough familiarity with the personality of the dreamer, such as sometimes came into use because of an overestimation of the sphere of validity of "lexica" of symbols, is absurd by its

very nature. According to Adler, all such an interpretation can hope to attain is the truth content of
the age-old popular custom of finding in dreams lot-
tery numbers or the impending arrival of love let-
ters.

Psychotherapeutic Understanding of Human Nature

Individual psychology postulates an intuitive
understanding of human nature, but it has also provided all aids to support intuition with scientific apparatus. The questioning or the observation (which
is a silent questioning) of a person must be able to
follow a guide— a catechism, as it were— in which
there is room for suppositions. In all questioning
there is half a knowing, and purposive questioning
is possible only if one knows in advance what can
be expected of a person. Only a profound knowledge of human nature in its totality permits one to
shed light on the individual personality. The human
understanding of individual psychology derives
from a background scheme of human nature against
which the individuality of a particular person can
stand out.

The chief result of an evaluation of a personality, either sound or diseased, should be the determination of a person's attitude toward his fellowmen. To this end one must scan the *life front* of a
person, as it were, share in experiencing his position
in the social world, and illuminate it through questions. His attitude toward his parents, siblings, sub-
ordinates, superiors, equals, friends, lovers, and rel-
atives, toward those of the same nationality and
social class, and toward mankind generally— all this
adds up to a person's *character profile,* which in
equal measure reflects his self-esteem and his social

experience. Here it is, of course, necessary to know how expressions of a person's character are to be evaluated. The evaluator must, as it were, himself possess that higher morality which enables him to recognize a character defect. In a certain sense any attempt at understanding human nature puts the person making it to a moral test, and all he will understand is what values of attitude or character he himself is capable of achieving.

To divine a character is a big task, difficult enough to make psychological diagnostics a problem of great import. A trained diagnostician can get to the point where he can grasp another person's personality very quickly and almost unconsciously from small symptomatic acts, first impressions, and a dialogue with the person seeking counsel. The way a person enters a room and introduces himself, the way he talks or keeps silent, the way he sits, walks, or stands— for the person trained in understanding human nature all this can become a symptom language that expresses the structure of a personality.

What intuition does not yield must be cleared up by a sure technique of questioning. Where a character cannot be divined, it can be revealed through a *study of behavior*. Every character reveals itself in modes of behavior, for it is the real reason for this behavior. The circumstances of a life keep changing, but in the face of every new life situation a person's self-assessment— which results from such factors as his ability to make contacts, his judgments and prejudices, and his experience of values—will give rise to a certain action. Human activity cannot be mathematically calculated in advance, but if one knows a person's "life plan," one will be able to understand his every action or inaction at least ex post facto, even though one may be unable to predict it: "If my attitude toward life were like his, then I would hardly have been able to act differently." Here one must also know that a person's reactions by no means form a disconnected conglomerate but rather a relatively uniform personality structure, a unified "world design," as the existentialists put it, or, in the language of individual psychology, a typical *Gangart* (gait) toward the problems of life, a personal guideline, a personality ideal that consciously and unconsciously strives to be actualized. To the initiate this personal guideline is revealed by all sorts of manifestations of life with such clarity that one can rule out any risk of error. In doubtful cases the psychological neophyte may derive enlightenment from a dictum of Adler by which he wished to teach his pupils to focus not so much on words but on actual behavior: "Don't watch his mouth; watch his hands."

What kind of behavior should the psychologist and judge of human nature evaluate in particular? Of the great variety of psychological material that has already been mentioned, individual psychology regards the *behavior within the course of a life* as especially characteristic. The way someone has lived or fashioned his life, the way he has met the difficulties posed to him by life, the way he has mastered or foundered on personal or universal situations— all these findings yield the most comprehensive picture of a personality and character structure in that they present a human being on the basis of the way he has shaped his life.

Within the framework of the questioning of a person in the spirit of individual psychology the following questions will be of significance:

What experiences were encountered in early childhood? Character of the mother and the father; what was the relationship to them? Pampering or a strict upbringing? Any behavioral peculiarities as a child, such as long-standing uncleanliness, refusal of food, thumb-sucking, bed-wetting, or anxiety reactions? Behavior toward siblings: only child, youngest, oldest, middle child, boy among girls or girl among boys? Were the siblings loved, hated, superior, or inferior? Favored or neglected by the parents? Kindergarten and school: sociable or isolated, quiet or lively? Accomplishments: industrious, dutiful, ambitious or indolent, negligent? Experiences with teachers: strict or good teachers, situations of punishment? Attitude toward a vocational choice: a clear choice or indistinct wishful thoughts? What occupation was chosen? Achievements in the occupational environment? Work satisfaction or dissatisfaction? Tendencies toward advancement? Awakening of sexuality: When? Told the facts of life or scared off? When and to what extent? Masturbation? When first love relationship, first sexual contact? What instinctual behavior dominates, what attitude toward the other sex, toward sexual intercourse? Frequency, potency, any deviations from the norm? Physical health and general sense of life: medical diagnosis? Childhood illnesses and their psychic processing? Fear of illness or death? Moods, feelings: optimism or pessimism? Intellectual level: intellectual abilities, educational level etc.; attitude toward religious, political, or philosophical questions? Dominant character: ambition, vanity, envy, avarice, hatred, anxiety, melancholia, compassion, social interest etc.; feelings such as inferiority or self-conceit?

The above scheme is necessarily incomplete. Basically, it is a flexible set of questions that must be intuitively adapted to the realities of each individual case. The psychologist and judge of human nature must sense where there is a productive problem and where it pays, as it were, to dig more deeply and do more detailed questioning. Such a diagnosis has the inestimable advantage of being able to take the form of an informal conversation. If a relationship of trust develops between the questioner and the questioned, the latter will gladly and sometimes unreservedly report about his experiential world. Here it is frequently found that a person will readily give a presentation of his life, evidently because it gives him a feeling of relief to tell another person listening with interest and understanding about his experiences and sufferings. In a certain sense such an existential confession, evoked by psychological questioning, contains a therapeutic factor. As he tells his story, the storyteller gains detachment from his problems that were a burden on him when he kept them to himself. The psychological questioning must, of course, always obey the laws of tact, and as it proceeds it must gradually and considerately turn to more intimate spheres. A question that would be justifiably rejected as indiscreet at the beginning of the conversation may a bit later on assume an entirely casual character. Care should be taken to discuss every problem, even the most intimate type, with a kind of sympathetic and yet matter-of-fact interest.

In this connection an ethical question arises. To know and understand human beings is, in the final analysis, not a problem of object-centered practice but one of man-centered ethos. This is what differentiates every deeper knowledge of human nature from the artful shrewdness or judgment of such persons as waiters, salesmen, and doormen. In the latter situation a person is looked at from a certain perspective, and accordingly he yields only this perspective— namely, what and how much can this person be sold? But the essential nature of a person can be grasped only by someone who has studied him for his own sake. Perhaps a basic understanding cannot even be separated from the desire or the inclination to help another person, to enable him to actualize his true nature. Knowledge of human na-

ture must not become a party game or a superficial
entertainment in which one shows his neighbor his
"mistakes" or unmasks him. Nor must it become a
vehicle of self-conceit that makes a person believe
he is exempt from his own insufficiencies because of his insight into the deficiencies of others.
It may sound moralistic, but one can really understand people only to the extent that one loves them,
and one will love them better if one understands
them better. The basic feeling of the genuine judge
of human nature must be respect for the other personality, an attitude free from judgmental and moralistic intentions. Nothing is harder for a person
than a capacity for such an unprejudiced encounter.
This is the origin of the psychological connection
that the good judges of human nature are those who
have themselves been caught up in the great entanglements of guilt, temptation, or inner distress
and have consequently been rendered conciliatory
and gentle—those who have experienced at first
hand the value of a human being, no matter which
existential error may be causing him to suffer.

5

Individual Psychological Theory of Education

The Educational Aim of Individual Psychology

No other pioneer of depth psychology has concerned himself with the problem of education as thoroughly as Adler. While Freud counted education, next to healing and ruling, among the "impossible occupations" and Jung early on turned to the eminently speculative problems of the "second half of life," Adler always clearly realized that educational practice constitutes the most valuable touchstone for any psychological theory. Since the theory of neurosis deals with all the conditions that cause psychological maldevelopment in childhood, it logically results in principles of psychological prophylaxis which must be applied in education. Experiences with mental patients pointed the way to a definition of the aim and method of pedagogical activity. Adler was the first to draw comprehensive conclusions for influencing children through education from depth psychology's understanding of human nature.

All of Adler's writings as well as those of his pupils are informed by an educational optimism which contrasts gratifyingly with the resigned and fainthearted creeds of our schools. *"L'éducation peut tout!"* [Education can do anything!] This slogan of Claude Andrien Helvétius could serve as the

motto of the educational thought of individual psychology, for it represents the view that all important
character traits of a person are dependent on what
happens in his education. Thus a psychologically
correct pedagogy is the prime requisite for the safe-
guarding of mental health. It alone can guarantee
that a child will grow up to be a valuable and productive human being.

The educational aim of individual psychology
emerges from its recognition of those factors in
human life and traditional education that impede
development. Since every psychological disturbance arises from isolation from one's fellowmen and
anxiety-laden egocentricity, every effort must be
made to integrate a growing person into the life of
the community as an aspiring and active member.
Courage and fitness for living are fundamental qualities which must be systematically nurtured. If a
pupil is enabled to assume responsibility for himself
and his fellowmen, the most important demand of
education has been activated in him. When this happens, the educational efforts of others have led to
self-education, the "unending task" which must be
continued for a lifetime.

The human community is the source of the rules
of life and of education. For individual psychology,
however, education for the community certainly
does not mean the adaptation of a young person to
an existing communal form. This usually is the unquestioningly accepted intent of every traditional
pedagogy which contents itself with assimilating a
person into the existing existential and cultural
structure, almost invariably in the belief that it already constitutes a high point of evolution. Cultural
criticism based on individual psychology does not,
however, admit of such a narrow viewpoint. The
goal which education should make children strive

for is not the wretched present state of cultural development but the ideal community of the future, which, as idea and inspiration, is the long-term objective of any humane endeavor. This is the meaning of Adler's statement: "It is our task to develop ourselves and our children into instruments of social progress."

Education for freedom thus is the guiding idea of individual psychological pedagogy. After what has already been said it need hardly be emphasized that this freedom has nothing to do with the liberalistic principle "*Laissez faire, laissez aller.*" Arbitrariness and lack of restraint are forms of unfree action; the economic life and the social structure of the past have postulated the tragic error that real freedom lies only in self-assertion at the expense of others. It is on this principle that capitalism, militarism, authoritarianism, and other harmful features of our communal life are based. Almost all ideologies of our epoch are still pervaded by the deleterious spirit of the will to power on which individual psychology has so resolutely declared war.

A free personality is conceivable only on the assumption that a sense of human fellowship has developed in it. We can count on freedom and creative energy to the degree that this sense of fellowship is developed. This makes *ability to cooperate* the most important goal of education in the spirit of individual psychology. Cooperation, however, means not only a working together but an emotional integration into the mainstream of communal life, of which every individual is the heir and continuator. Putting it in popular terms, Adler said that a child should be trained to become a "good team player." He aptly characterized the great army of psychological failures as opponents whom an improper education has turned not into fellowmen but into "counter-men." The term *Mitmenschlichkeit* (fellow feeling) includes all other designations for positive development. Only on the basis of this concept can virtue and efficiency, responsibility and creativity be understood. It is the *sine qua non* of social living and any self-actualization within a culture; it brings people together by teaching them "to see with someone else's eyes, to hear with someone else's ears, to feel with someone else's heart."

The real driving force of the educational practice of individual psychology is the impulse of social ethics. It presupposes that a child possesses the capacity for education and development, but it clearly emphasizes that the social interest potentially present in every child needs to be carefully cultivated by his environment. It is true that man is a social being, but his sociability is not safeguarded by instincts—he is not a herd animal but a social being. The lack of instinctive integration into the social environment imposes upon everyone the task of working toward his own form of fellow feeling. What an animal receives without effort a human must acquire through trial and error. On his way to the realization of social values he can, to a varying extent, stray from the right road, particularly if he is influenced in an improper and uncomprehending way. He can strive to compensate for his weakness and imperfection as a child through goals which necessarily put him in conflict with the biological realities of his life, his connection with his fellowmen, and evolution in general.

Hence education must also guide the meaningful development of all active energies in a person. It must be an aid to compensation, which early on channels a child's urge for growth and perfection in the proper directions. Like life itself, those take myriad forms, but basically they have one thing in common: they are in line with the general good. Individual psychology recognizes no real conflict between self-development and usefulness to the community. Only a superficial, i.e., neurotic, observer will see in devotion to the community and the tasks arising from it the danger of a loss of self; actually, an individual can find himself only if he is absorbed in a Thou or in a We. Despite its clear emphasis on absolute noncoercion in education, individual psychology favors guidance for a child, and from the beginning such guidance aims at instilling in the child the makings of a positive social conscience. It must not confine itself to exerting good influences, but must also see how the child takes these up and utilizes them. When a child's weakness and ignorance make him view resistance against his educators and thus also against his own further development as a way out of his oppressive situation, he must be given the courage to strike out on the road to real progress. Erwin Wexberg was right when he formulated it this way: "To educate means, in concrete terms, nothing but to encourage."

If one defines the aim of education in the spirit of individual psychology as the systematic promotion of "independence, courage, sense of responsibility and community" (Wexberg), one basically proclaims the ideal of an *education for freedom*. In point of fact, the humanism of individual psychology appears at its finest in its pedagogical theory and practice, which are among the most valuable accomplishments of depth psychology. Adler thereby made one of the most promising and most positive contributions to the fulfillment of Nietzsche's high-minded prophecy that some day "a time will come whose only thought will be education."

As we have already mentioned, Adler referred

to the problem of education in all his writings. It was his aim to train parents for their educative function, for he hoped that an improvement in education would bring about a genuine prophylaxis for neuroses. He realized, of course, that it is not possible to learn how to educate children through theoretical instruction alone. An educator educates not so much through what he knows but through what he is. Therefore depth psychology endeavored at a very early date to teach child psychology within the framework of a large-scale *training of parents*. Only if one helps the parents to become more mature, more knowledgeable, and more capable of forming interpersonal relationships, only if one eliminates sources of disturbance from marriage and sexuality, and only if the parents learn how to lead a more productive life in a communal spirit is there a chance that an adequate environment will be created for the child, one in which he can develop his energies and abilities in the direction of sociability. More than all other depth psychologists, Adler emphasized that education must always involve the self-education of the educator. To educate a child is perhaps the most difficult task that can be imposed upon a human being. It requires sound knowledge, poise, patience, sensitivity, and genuine devotion to the goal of education: to help a developing young person build his personality. Many educators do not take this task seriously enough, and often they do not even know that they have a lot to learn. They proceed from the assumption that they are able to educate others because they were once educated themselves. So it happens that every generation transmits the character flaws and attitudinal defects it has acquired to the next generation. For a psychotherapist it is frequently a shock to see how in some families certain psychological deformities almost become a tradition that extends over generations, giving rise to an erroneous impression that heredity and disposition are responsible.

Heredity and Education

To what extent is an educator in a position to shape the character and personality of his pupil? Before the era of depth psychology the assumption undoubtedly prevailed that the essential psychological factors of life are present at birth in the form of inherited dispositions. Under the influence of biological evolutionism, the idea of heredity was taken over by psychology without examination. Lombroso's catchwords about the "born" criminal and the "born" prostitute are symbols of an epoch which derived from sources in religion and natural science the postulate that all psychological qualities are determined by disposition. Psychoanalysis is still dominated by the theory of heredity, and it shrouds many problems of faulty human development in the impenetrable fog of "constitutional anomaly."

Individual psychology categorically rejects the assumption that psychological characteristics are inherited. In his study of the neurotic constitution Adler found that all character traits of a person can be meaningfully connected with his situation in childhood and youth. The explainability of human behavior on the basis of a guideline adopted in childhood under the pressure of conditions is one of the most significant findings of depth psychological research. In studying healthy or abnormal lives, depth psychology is able to show that human character traits are acquired rather than inborn. Character proves to be a *social reaction*, an attempt to respond to the questions of life as they present themselves to the individual in his environment. It must be noted that Adler's teachings here are not based on a theory of environment, even though they admit that the (social) environment has an extraordinary power to shape a growing person. But in its conception of character as a person's "answer and attitude" to his situation in early childhood, Adler's theory affirms human freedom and self-development, which creatively utilize the existing material of biological and environmental conditions. The attitude which a person assumes toward the inner and outer conditions of his life constitutes the special nature of his character. Character is nothing but that mold which a person assumes under the impression of experiences in childhood. As guideline and life plan this constitutes an attempt to cope with the problems of human communal living on the analogy of childhood impressions or modes of behavior practiced (and made automatic) in childhood. As a product of psychological development, character is not static and unchangeable. It can undergo a systematic alteration, especially with the aid of depth psychological character analysis, which uncovers even the uncomprehended motives of behavior. The transformation of character is possible if the automatism of unconscious or uncomprehended reactions is disrupted by self-knowledge.

Individual psychology thus does not regard the similarity of character traits in parents and children as proof of heredity but as an indication of the child's imitative ability. Certainly a child's emotional and intellectual growth depends on his imitating the behavior of adults. Then, too, a parent's character trait is a force that incessantly affects the child and conveys the parent's view of life to him; thus it is not surprising that the child patterns his attitude after such a character trait. Neuroses and mental illnesses, too, are not transmitted through the inherited constitution but through the influence of the latently or manifestly ill educator.

In this spirit Kretschmer's constitution theory must also be reduced to manageable proportions. This theory proceeded from the relationship of certain mental illnesses to specific body types. From this it derived the scheme that rotund persons tend to alternate lively and depressed moods, while slender people are disposed to abrupt changes in mood and related reactions. Kretschmer was describing manifestations of temperament, and thus it amounted to an astonishing generalization when he entitled his well-known work *Body Structure and Character*. This imprecision involved a great deal of unclarity, which has impeded discussion of the problem to this day. Adler at first was ready to view Kretschmer's typology as a valuable extension of his doctrine of organ inferiority; later, however, he rejected all typologies as "schematizing," as an intellectual shortcut that sacrifices what is best about psychological knowledge to a desire for stereotypes and pigeonholes. In his uniqueness and originality an individual usually disproves the most sophisticated typologies, and temperament and character countless times contradict the prejudiced notion that it is possible to draw far-reaching conclusions from body types.

Individual psychology believes that character and temperament are not the only acquired personality factors into which biological and other elements can enter only as building material; within Adler's doctrine, intelligence also is a dimension that is dependent on the life-style. If one follows Wilhelm Stern in defining intelligence as the ability of the mind to adapt or readjust to new situations, or if one describes it in the spirit of individual psy-

chology as the fruitful coping with life (the "con-
ducting of life"), it becomes evident that character
and intelligence are intertwined. Provided that biological feeblemindedness is ruled out, individual
psychology postulates that all developmental possibilities are present in every child. "Anybody can
accomplish anything," according to Adler. Intelligence is the result of a training that will be successful primarily when through education a character has acquired the "openness to the world" that
is inherent in social interest. Usually this also is the
source of the courage which is expressed in every
exertion of the intelligence. Only those can overcome the resistance of the material and attain to understanding and profundity who are imbued with a
desire to contribute to the general welfare. Adler
called the intelligence arising from the social attitude *common sense* and drew a distinction between
it and the *private intelligence* of mentally ill persons, who place their resourcefulness in the service
of egocentric pseudoproblems. To a superficial observer such people may appear to be unintelligent,
as with feeblemindedness of psychological origin,
yet what is fundamentally disturbed is not the intelligence but the attitude toward life.

In light of this, individual psychology cannot
believe in innate *talent* either. In every achievement it recognizes the courage and the training
which, in the final analysis, are anchored in the productive personality. Talent and lack of talent are
superficial problems; anyone who digs more deeply
recognizes behind them a life history which, with
a certain inevitability, promotes the acquisition or
nonacquisition of qualities leading to achievement.
The paralyzing fatalism inherent in the talent delusion disregards the application and the effort with
which all talented people develop their abilities.

Here, too, education (and the subsequent self-education) must be assigned the primary role. The activities and values with which the child has his most important and most impressive experiences of success and through which he receives the greatest measure of recognition and affection become the unconscious motives guiding his endeavors. The greater the self-confidence and fellow feeling that have been aroused in the child, the more tenacious and more resolute will his endeavors be. Genius, as the extreme form of talent, is also a person's great effort to solve culturally significant problems. Schiller's statement that genius is perhaps only diligence is borne out by depth psychology if one adds that the diligence of a genius must be inspired by self-conquest in early childhood and a grandiose— though often greatly fluctuating—self-confidence.

In rejecting belief in heredity, individual psychology eliminates any educational pessimism of the kind that has had such deleterious consequences in the past. It thereby imposes a greater responsibility on the educator, but it also shows him new opportunities for pedagogical creativity. Finally, it opens up a free horizon for a child's self-actualization. Its faith in education not only is supported by theoretical arguments but also offers the best practical guarantee that all educational possibilities will be exploited. Only faith in the unlimited educability and malleability of human beings can be a basic precept and guiding star in educational practice.

Familial Education

The task of education belongs primarily among the functions of the family. In Adler's view, the family, even in what still is for the most part its very

imperfect form, is the best milieu in which a growing person can develop. (In his book *Individualpsychologie* E. Wexberg is inclined to give pride of
place to community education.) But one decisive
lack must be emphasized: the parents are by no
means prepared for their educative role. "Unfortunately there is no denying that parents are neither
good psychologists nor good teachers" (Adler, *Understanding Human Nature*). The need to change
this situation is all the more urgent because familial
education is the most important factor in structuring
the psychological life of a child. A child uses his
mother and father to develop his picture of the
world by fundamentally incorporating into his sense
of life his early experiences with these authoritative
persons, to whom he is relating. Hence it would be
of the greatest importance to give careful instruc-
tions to the parents regarding their educational activities. For individual psychology the education of
the educators is the best and most promising element of any system of pedagogy and psychology.

In line with what Pestalozzi recognized as early
as the eighteenth century, Adler assigned to the
mother a key position in the education of the child.
According to him, a child experiences his first fellow
human being in the mother. The relationship between mother and child, which psychoanalysis used
to be fond of describing by the deprecatory term
parasitism (on the child's part), was interpreted by
Adler in the sense of a symbiosis, a life companionship for the mutual benefit of those involved. It is
not simply that the child needs the mother; the
mother needs the child, too. As the mother satisfies
the child's need for affection, which manifests itself
at an early age and is a reflection of the social interest to awaken later, she soon receives expressions
of the child's affection which contribute to her well-

being and heighten the happiness of her mother-hood. Ideally speaking, the mother should afford her child the experience of absolute dependability. Her love nourishes the child's budding social interest. If one considers the enormous role that the kind and degree of people's social interest plays in their private and public lives, one can gauge the magnitude of the cultural achievement of mothers. This was one reason why Adler championed the absolute equality of women. Civilization hurts itself if it proclaims the delusive prejudice of male superiority and thus deprives a woman, whose enjoyment of life is diminished by traditional prejudices, of her zestfulness in her sphere of life. Adler emphatically stated: "We probably owe the greater part of our human social interest and thus also the essential content of culture to this feeling of contact with the mother" (*The Science of Living*).

In this connection we should point out that the research of recent years has offered impressive documentation of this thesis. René Spitz of New York, a personal pupil of Freud, through extremely significant investigations clarified the extent to which the child is responsive to psychic influences from his environment in the first, unconscious stage of his life. It was possible to solve this problem mainly through observation of children in orphanages and foundling hospitals. These children, who despite adequate nutrition and hygiene had experienced a lack of mother love, displayed typical deficiency symptoms, and subsequent experiments showed that these were always caused by the missing factor of a maternal relationship. Children from an unloving environment are as a rule characterized by deficient development. They display more anxiety than normal children and seem to be constantly living—or vegetating—without any feeling of pleasure; not infrequently *affective neglect* causes, as early as the first year of life, a split in the child's personality, which may not be curable later on. These observations, which have made possible far-reaching conclusions about the genesis of neuroses and mental illnesses, also make it easy to deduce the magnitude of the mother's influence.

As far as individual psychology is concerned, the mother has a twofold task vis-à-vis her child: in a first phase she should direct the child's social interest to herself; at a second developmental stage, however, she should cause the child to extend this interest to the other members of the family. She must not impede this process through a pampering or possessive attitude. The father in particular, who in the nature of things does not come into the child's field of vision until later, must start his relationship with the child as a friend and comrade. The fact that his daily work gives him fewer opportunities for contact with his child should not prevent him from imparting to the growing child in the brief episodes of their togetherness a sense of his benevolence and understanding. The father, too, plays an incalculable role in the psychological household environment of the child. His economic and social function gives the child a first guidance for his later tasks in life. In our patriarchal culture the father also largely radiates the significance of a reliable support for both boys and girls. As the former becomes aware of his sexual identity, the father also becomes a clear model that enables the boy to make a preliminary assessment of his future path in life. Individual psychology utterly rejects the psychoanalytic speculation which ascribes to the boy primary feelings of envy and competition and to the girl sensual feelings of affection for the father. Normally, a child should have equally strong and sound ties to both parents. If these ties appear in the form of a claim to exclusivity (which psychoanalysis misinterprets as Oedipus complex), they are the artificial product of a pampering, unhealthy upbringing.

From his family the child receives the inner strength and independence to cope with the difficulties of his life. This, however, is the case only if the familial education is not psychologically a failure. The countless psychological failures, reflected in anything from neurosis to mental illness, are always characterized by the fact that the family has not done justice to its educational task. Individual psychology emphasizes that parents educate not only knowingly and intentionally but also unknowingly and unintentionally. Thus the very stability and meaningfulness of the marital relationship is an educational factor of the first order. The atmosphere which a married couple creates through the way in which it lives together has a stronger and more lasting effect on the children than the isolated educational acts that follow momentary moods or inspirations. Accordingly, a psychologically correct education begins with a sound marriage. Only a happy or inwardly satisfied woman will be able to counter the difficulties of her maternal role with a well-tempered measure of love and understanding.

Sex education, too, still belongs in the familial realm. This aspect has never been neglected by individual psychology, though Adler's rejection of the psychoanalytic generalizations about the sex drive gave rise to the erroneous notion that his teachings underestimated the importance of the instinct-directed part of life. In point of fact, the careful preparation of a child for life is advocated in this area as well. The parents' unembarrassed attitude toward their bodily existence, as well as their overcoming of prudery and bashfulness about their nudity, constitutes a bit of sex education even before the child has learned the words pertaining to this problem. At a later date, biological and especially psychological information about the relationships between the sexes should be imparted—within a child's capacity, but as clearly and forthrightly as possible. Needless to say, the present equipment of parents for these problems is totally inadequate in this respect as well, and so the school should take their place in telling a child the facts of life.

Sibling relationships, another educational factor of great psychological import, will be the subject of the next section.

Position in the Sibling Order

One of Adler's most important discoveries concerns the influence of a person's position in the sibling order on his subsequent emotional development. The situation in which a child grows up is exemplary for the attitude toward life which he formulates early on and by which he lives more or less unconsciously. Next to all the other factors that have already been mentioned, a child's relationship with his siblings is of the greatest importance. Although individual cases must always be taken into account, Adler virtually sets up a typology according to which certain character types may, with some degree of probability, be associated with certain situations in early childhood.

One such type is the *youngest child*. With striking frequency he is described in fairy tales and legends as having a special position. This is a reflection of the special situation which the youngest child as a rule finds in the family atmosphere. As the smallest and the one most in need of help, his parents sometimes treat him differently from the way they treat his siblings, who are already better at coping with life and in whose midst the youngest child occupies a privileged position. This can give rise to the evolution of a "nestling"— that is, a person who is spoiled and sheltered by his parents and develops severe feelings of inferiority, shrinking from the demands of life or evading them. On the other hand, however, the youngest child may feel impelled to redouble his efforts to catch up with his siblings, who have surpassed him. He can become a "sprinter" whose entire psychological movement is aimed at getting ahead of others. But as his aptitude for greater achievement grows, so does his susceptibility to emotional illness. Thus one finds among persons of this type severe failure alongside genuine greatness.

According to Adler, the *oldest child* is in a special situation as well. Since this child is usually called upon to take care of younger siblings, he or she learns at an early age to shoulder responsibility. Even though the tradition of a bygone age that regarded the oldest boy as the son and heir of a house no longer looms large today, he is nevertheless frequently in a leading position, and this may have a favorable effect on his psychological development. Unless he is overburdened by his educational situation, he enjoys a relatively large amount of leeway and includes the younger children whom he has to take care of in his social interest, which gives him a good chance to develop it. Under authoritarian conditions, however, such as prevail almost everywhere in our culture, there is a temptation for the oldest child to develop his participation in parental power in authoritarian fashion. According to Adler's observation, oldest children often have a conservative character, which can make them worshipers of authority and order.

The *only child* also is a well-defined type. His situation must in general be regarded as rather unfavorable. Since he has no competitors, he is, so to speak, completely at the mercy of his parents' love. Hence he usually gets into a position of pampering, which promotes the development of severe feelings of inferiority. This is especially due to the fact that because of the lack of siblings, the gulf between the child and the physical size and complete authority of his parents is all but unbridgeable. (The child feels he would have a good chance to get the better of any siblings.) An inevitable consequence of pampering is the inner dependence which such children carry over into their later adult life. They are deeply discouraged, and after a few reverses life seems hostile to them and they have trouble overcoming their basic attitude, which in the face of their childhood situation includes a resigned or parasitic outlook on life.

As he does for the youngest child, Adler names a tendency for the *second child*: to surpass others and to push vigorously ahead. Anyone who constantly has a superior sibling in view will, under favorable circumstances, feel impelled to emulate and outdo him. The stimulus for this, of course, is present only if the older child is not too far ahead. It also depends on which child the educator bestows his love upon. One frequently makes the observation that the second child is more ambitious in this regard as well and can obtain more affection for himself with his behavior—until he himself may be "dethroned" by a younger child who comes pushing along.

More complicated positions are also relevant for the development of typical reactions. It is in the nature of things that an only boy with a number of sisters or an only girl with a number of brothers faces a difficult situation, and it will not be surprising if severe inferiority feelings based on gender develop. Boys who have a sister of almost the same age might be shocked in puberty by the fact that at this stage of development girls generally mature more rapidly.

This Adlerian typology is a valuable aid if one always keeps in mind that Adler did not regard general rules or guidelines as binding. As far as he was concerned, they were only supposed to illuminate the area in which the individual case, the only essential thing in practice, is found or missed. At any rate, the question as to the position in the sibling order is indispensable for characterology and psychotherapy. In the latter in particular, it can be shown that every psychological ailment contains elements of the position that the patient occupied among his siblings in early childhood. An understanding of the laws governing these connections promotes a rapid orientation as to the motives of the psychological disturbance. The character portrait of a person becomes more graphic if the childhood pattern, which he has unconsciously carried over into his adult life from his position within the family as a whole, becomes visible in his present situation.

Educational Attitudes: Pampering, Strictness and Severity, Antiauthoritarianism

The childhood history of every neurotic person indicates that the basic attitude of his educators did not meet his real emotional needs. A disposition to a psychological disturbance or illness is produced not so much by isolated traumas, as psychoanalysis believed, as by the total atmosphere, the climate of an upbringing. Individual psychology describes primarily two faulty attitudes of traditional education which become a source of psychological failure. Ed-

ucational errors stem from parents' deficient information about a child's nature and mode of reaction.
They are bound up with ancient prejudices about
people and human education, and they are also
manifestations of the parents' character as expressed
in a specific educational method.

Adler regarded *pampering* as the most important root of an arrested psychological development.
The "tropical heat" or "hothouse atmosphere" of a
pampered upbringing is not designed to promote a
child's courage to face life or his social interest. The
excessive affection of the mother, which is seldom
free of an admixture of hunger for power, fear of life,
and frustration, has a paralyzing effect on a child's
urge to grow up and become independent. The misfortune of pampered children lies in their encoun-
tering too little resistance on their path, and thus
they are not in a position to get to know their faculties and test their strength. The educator who
clears the obstacles from their path because he
thinks he must protect them to an inordinate degree
deprives them of a chance to train for real life.
Hence pampered children early on start living in an
imaginary world and adopt a method of living which
is tailored to the person who pampers them but is
unsuitable for life within the community. In most
cases, pampering deepens a child's fear of life and
feelings of inferiority, and the child absorbs the anxieties of his overly solicitous educator in "halluci-
natory" fashion, as it were. This becomes the child's
attitude toward life, and we find that all pampered
children feel they are living in enemy country because they are not strong enough to endure reverses
when they are on their own. Hence they sooner or
later display marked tendencies toward isolation,
use trickery in an attempt to restore the pampering
situation of childhood, and even in adulthood retain

the parasitic attitude that was instilled in them in childhood. A certain thought pattern that stems from being pampered is the cause of neurosis and frequently also of perversion, addiction, criminality, and all other character defects. In line with this pattern the individual concerned believes that whenever he faces difficulties in life he must exploit someone else's help and retreat into self-indulgence. In the final analysis, this basic tendency derives from the failure of the child's education to instill in him a desire to cooperate and to make him take pleasure in such cooperation. The type of person who grows up amidst immoderate and senseless demonstrations of affection almost always fails to adjust to life—primarily because he has not been able to develop sufficient social interest. His failure is the logical consequence of his more or less great cowardice in the face of life and of his undeveloped understanding of the communal nature of life's tasks. Adler's psychopathological experience led him to state emphatically that "there is no greater evil than the pampering of children with all its consequences" (*Der Sinn des Lebens*).

But just as harmful as pampering is its apparent opposite, *severity and strictness* in education. This attitude, too, is based on misconceptions about a child's psyche and on deficiencies in the parental character. Religious notions of the original sinful nature of man have contributed a great deal to hardening an educator's readiness to adopt a harsh and unyielding stance. The authoritarian structure of our social order—as for example in the spheres of politics, the economy, and militarism—also promotes the pedagogical mentality that would like to turn a child into a vassal (see Heinrich Mann's novel *Der Untertan*, translated into English as *Little Superman*), who can later be used in the hierarchi-

cal social system. The unfortunate thing about a
harsh and strict upbringing is that it substantially
increases the distance between the parents and the
child. If a child is to have the courage to face life,
he needs to feel, first and foremost, that he is sheltered and loved in the family environment. When
the parents place primary stress on the child's sub-
ordination, the growing child's need for affection
generally is not satisfied, and thus the child does
not learn to make full use of his capacity to love.
Authoritarian pedagogy usually turns into a drill
which exacts from the child modes of behavior that
he inwardly does not approve of. This also causes
the child to be largely isolated from his environment. He may attain to a cautious modus vivendi
with this environment, but he will not integrate it
into his emotions. The consequence of this is an
emotional isolation, which in later life may appear
as inhibition, pessimism, and negativism. This, too,
is a starting point of psychological maldevelopments
ranging from general character defects to perversions, criminality, and mental illness. The parental
attitudes that fall under the rubric of severity and
strictness— imperiousness, faultfinding, lovelessness— hit a child at his most vulnerable spot by
shattering his feeling of security and crippling his
capacity for love. The type of person created by authoritarian education (and largely the basic type of
our era) is merely a caricature of what a human being
ought to be. For freedom it substitutes submissiveness, for creative productivity a puppetlike existence, and for fellow feeling the "war of everyone
against everyone" which completely poisons interpersonal relationships.

One frequently encounters an education con-
sisting of a mixture of pampering and strictness, depending on the parents' mood or the child's behav-

ior. It need hardly be emphasized that excessive pampering is not made right by subsequent severity; errors can hardly be corrected by different errors. The problem of punishment, which used to be unquestioningly accepted as one of the valid educational methods, also belongs in this context. As we have already mentioned, individual psychology categorically denies the right to punish by demonstrating that all disorders and behavior defects of a child derive from the improper influence of the parents. A stubborn child, a child who is unwilling to learn, or one who has become a delinquent is appealing to his parents to correct their educational attitude or to have it reviewed by someone else. A child's maldevelopment cannot be cured by traditional punitive methods. Beatings and other punishments are primitive and crude reactions on the part of the educator, and their effects are far worse than the adult suspects; in fact, they constitute an educational capitulation which the child perceives as a severe breach of trust.

Individual psychology espouses an *antiauthoritarian education*, which regards an adult as a friend and supporter of the child. The best guarantee that the growing child will thrive is the maintenance by his parents of a uniformly benevolent and instructive attitude. In this spirit, abnormal attitudes on the part of the child must be regarded as errors rather than malevolence. In every person who is brought up in authoritarian fashion there is a tendency to sit in judgment over others and condemn them, and this imperils the sound relationship between parents and child. Dropping any claim to authority removes the possibility of the child rebelling against his educators. "A defiant child," Adler claimed, "defies only authority . . . Those who wish to avoid a defiant attitude should not train a child to obey"

["Trotz und Gehorsam," in *Heilen und Bilden*, pp. 84 ff.] If the child is to become a good team player in life, he must from an early age grow up in an atmosphere of equality and equal rights. This does not preclude gentle guidance; in fact, it virtually requires it. By appealing as early as possible to the child's budding reason and cooperative capacity, such guidance will strengthen the child's sense of community and lay the foundation for a social view of life which constitutes the most decisive protection of mental health.

Childhood Disorders

Adler adduced cogent arguments for his viewpoint that a person's character is formed by education rather than heredity. The sense of life and the attitude toward life which a child will acquire are, so to speak, in the parents' hands. Asocial and undesirable character traits are not predetermined by fate but are responses by the child to unpleasant things in his education and environment which a psychotherapist can often recognize after just a brief evaluation.

Thus the educator must constantly guard against the child becoming power-hungry or discouraged. The child should learn to obey the social rules but not to follow them slavishly. His character should be that of a fellow player in the game of life. But this also means discouraging those character traits which generally have negative effects, such as ambition, vanity, arrogance, mistrust, cantankerousness, envy, jealousy, timidity, and depression. According to Adler, an educator definitely has the power to make of his charge an honorable and courageous person. To be sure, this is not easy in the civilization in which we are living because our cultural conditions are informed by the deleterious spirit of prejudice, anomie, and cheap intoxication with power. Nevertheless, an educator must not give up. His influence begins early enough for him to immunize the child against some of the pervasive defects of the cultural environment. It is the great achievement of depth psychology that it has made everyone aware of the importance of the childhood years for the development and growth of a person. But a great deal of educational work remains to be done before "psychological illiteracy" can be overcome. It is particularly in questions of education that ignorance, traditional stupidity, and naiveté as well as dogmatism exert a disastrous influence.

As in a test, a child's behavior unmistakably demonstrates the skill or the failure of his educators. The psychologically correct guidance of the growing child yields the rich reward of the child's readiness to be educated and to comply with the demands of the community. Without pressure or compulsion, a well-educated child is inclined to acquire independence in growing measure and to attain in his physical and psychic functions that degree of cooperation which is widely termed *normality*. If, however, there is an improper education which unnecessarily aggravates the child's feelings of inferiority and which pushes the correspondingly incited striving for superiority to the useless side of life, those disturbances which have generally been grouped together as *childhood disorders* soon manifest themselves. These forms of childhood nervousness, which include also all kinds of so-called maladjustments, are actually childhood neuroses, which adults erroneously evaluate as a child's lack of will or as an arrested development that the child can still outgrow by himself.

The approach of individual psychology facili-

tates a deeper understanding of childhood disorders. All these behavioral anomalies are based on a
child's fear of life which has been considerably ag-
gravated by an educator's psychologically unsound
measures. The very stubborness of the child, which
has been referred to in the proceding chapter, is a
reaction to an environment that hurts the child's
personality with its unjustified claim to power. According to Charlotte Bühler, the so-called age of defiance normally comes in the third year of life, but
individual psychology has found that it is not the
defiance but the self-awareness that is develop-
mentally determined. Only if the awakening ego of
the child encounters insensate resistance on the part
of his environment does his sound self-will become
perverted into a negativism that can represent an
early form of later mental illness. The educator who
forcibly turns this defiance into submissive behavior even more dependably prepares the soil for future neuroses. Next to related phenomena such as
inhibition and shyness, submissiveness is almost invariably a sign of severe discouragement, which always manifests itself when problems in life arise
that cannot be mastered with the model child ster-
eotype.

A child's anxiety also has a physiological foundation, but in the development of the child it frequently constitutes a neurosis-causing factor. Children who are pampered, raised in loveless fashion,
or are not given enough scope to develop their independence early on discover anxiety as a means of
arousing the attention of their environment and
making this environment cater to them. If one ex-
amines the social meaning of the anxiety affect, it
becomes evident that it can be used to keep the
surrounding persons on the alert; their social interest exacts greater considerateness from them, and

thus the anxious person gains a position which seemingly raises his rank. Here it is a matter of *dominance through weakness*, which the young person attains by exploiting his own infirmity as well as the compassion of others. As we have already mentioned, this causal connection applies to every neurosis, at least to some extent.

The other childhood disorders also follow this principle. The child's resistance to his education springs from his inferiority complex, for which his educators do not permit him to compensate in a socially sound manner. A child who tells lies immediately leads us to surmise that he must be surrounded by adults he fears. An unafraid child who can trust his parents completely and is sure of their understanding will never need to lie, unless his fantasizing leads him inadvertently to confuse the boundaries between reality and dreaming. The chastisement that is inflicted on the liar because his parents are moralistic truth fanatics tends to anchor untruthfulness permanently in the child's character. Truthfulness is merely a function of courage and social interest; a child can be taught to be truthful only by enhancing and strengthening these qualities. Here, as everywhere else, moralizing will lead only to pseudosuccesses which flatter the educator's self-righteousness.

A child who steals is also an emotionally ill child. Individual psychology proceeds from the premise that only a person who feels robbed will steal. As a rule, this involves problems of the loss of affection, for which a child tries to compensate by his misdemeanors. The oldest child who feels that a little sibling has robbed him of his mother may resort to such an action to proclaim his protest against the changed family situation. The stolen candy or money then constitutes the sad resources which the child uses to restore his disturbed self-esteem. Here, too, educational therapy must, in Adler's metaphor, "extinguish the fire and not just dispel the smoke." The little "thief" is not a real delinquent; he simply uses a child's methods to eliminate his painful misfortune. If he is publicly exposed as a thieving and dishonest character, there is every prospect that the childish folly will be perpetuated. The watchword of individual psychology, however, is healing and not punishing, and this is based on the premise that one must build golden bridges for the problem child on which he can make his peace with a community he perceives as hostile.

Nibbling, nail biting, and nose picking are other symptomatic acts which can be traced to deep-seated conflicts. In the case of every bad habit of a child, one must remember that the educator probably prohibited a child hundreds of times from indulging it, and from this it becomes readily apparent that defiance is the motive of these childhood disorders. That is why there is no point in trying to remove the superficial symptom. The defiance underlying them will easily be able to create other modes of expression which will sustain the child's struggle against his educators.

Bed-wetting and stuttering are childhood disorders whose significance is great primarily because they hit education at its most vulnerable spots: cleanliness and linguistic development. Here, too, we are dealing with childhood neuroses, with an outcry of a helpless child protesting against an adult's lack of understanding. In such cases Adler spoke of an *organ dialect*; one can use one's organs, or their impaired activity, to say that one does not feel at home in this world. Usually these symptoms are triggered by evident psychological overstrain. A child supplanted by a little sibling may start to wet his bed so as to emphasize his own childishness, thereby expressing, as it were, that he himself is still little and in need of care (bed-wetting being equivalent to "crying through one's bladder"). A stutterer indicates through his speech movement how hard it is for him to reach the other person. His disturbance invariably impedes the others as well; those upon whom the stutterer forces his pace of communication have to listen longer and more carefully. It is not traumatic experiences that cause stuttering, although such experiences may accompany the onset of the disturbance. What is more important, however, is that the feeling of inferiority, which seems ineluctable, holds on to some shock and exploits it in order to come to terms with the environment. The environment's interest in combatting the symptom leads to a retention of the stuttering, and in time a vicious circle develops: the stutterer is ashamed of his malady, and the more embarrassed he is, the less he is able to get over it. Fritz Künkel, a rather unoriginal pupil of Adler, coined for this the useful expression *Dressat* [acquired adjustment pattern; from *dressieren* (to train or drill)] a term that takes cognizance of the automatic nature of such dysfunctions.

Laziness, hot temper, nervous vomiting, lack of appetite, gluttony, indigestion, sexual precocity, and learning disabilities are some of the other childhood disorders which individual psychology directly traces back to a faulty education. Once a child adopts a stance of opposition to his educational environment, any of his tasks or functions can become a theater of war in which he carries on his fight against his parents. To put it succinctly, all these symptoms represent a "no" to the efforts of the educator. An unintelligent child's inability to learn is also frequently a product of education, systematic discouragement having led the child to conclude that withdrawal into complete passivity is the best solution to his otherwise insoluble tasks in life. This thesis is said to have been impressively confirmed in many schoools. In a special school for "backward" children P. Kaltenborn attempted to apply the individual psychological system of constant encouragement, and after a few years he was able to raise the achievement level of some of his pupils above that of normal pupils.

The curing of children beset by childhood disorders is accomplished through educational guidance which usually includes modest psychotherapy for the child and also for his parents. We shall give a more detailed account of the questions of individual psychological child guidance in connection with psychotherapeutic problems.

Individual Psychology and the School

In Adler's teachings the school ranks high in the emotional and intellectual development of the child. It is the first social test of the child, the first experiment that tells us how far the child's preparation for life has progressed. Here we have a thousand opportunities to correct a child's life-style which, under the influence of faulty parental education, has come into conflict with community life. To this end, however, the school must abandon mere didacticism and imparting of knowledge and unequivocally embrace development aid, that is, personality formation. For individual psychology the development of the social sense is the most important task of the school. The school should consider the imparting of knowledge as well as the training of abilities and capacity for work and achievement in terms of the goal of genuine human development; it should educate more than instruct, and in everything it does it should see to it that the pupil develops into a courageous and responsible human being.

At an early date Adler turned his full attention to the problems of schooling, and as a lecturer at the Pedagogical Institute of the City of Vienna he introduced teachers to individual psychology. His presentations of case histories of difficult school-children, as published principally in *Technik der Individualpsychologie* and *Individualpsychologie in der Schule*, are masterpieces of the psychological interview in which a child's faulty life-style is revealed to him and to his parents. From 1931 to 1934 Vienna had an individual psychological experimental school at which Adler's pupils (Ferdinand Birnbaum, later Oskar Spiel) translated the theoretical idea of a community school into practice. Socialistic Vienna promoted this extremely successful experiment, but unfortunately it was disrupted by Austrian fascism and National Socialism. After World War II Oskar Spiel revived this school and developed it into an institution highly respected in educational circles. His 1947 book *Am Schaltbrett der Erziehung* [At the Controls of Education] has served as a guide for the following remarks.

In the spirit of individual psychology, the school should be organized in such a way that a democratic school community can be realized in the greatest possible measure. It should offer the child a "training ground for social relatedness." Since its pupils are children whose character has already been formed, it must expect to find innumerable kinds of resistance in the pupils' attitude. Many children find it very difficult to integrate themselves among equals as equals. From their parental home they bring along attitudes toward their teachers and

the class community which have been drilled into
them, and these attitudes are bound to assert themselves. Oversubmissiveness or permanent opposition are the two opposite ends on a scale on which
there can be all sorts of maladjustments on the part
of a child. A teacher must not react to this with personal sensitivity or let his hurt pride come to the
fore. Everything depends on his having sufficient
psychological knowledge and pedagogical skill to
win over the child and bring out his community
spirit.

In a school run along the lines of individual
psychology, the coercive atmosphere of the old type
of school that emphasized learning by rote is completely eliminated. Discipline, the idol of traditional schools, is replaced by a flexible scheme that
aims at independence and encouragement. The
teacher gives up his position of authority and power
and steps into the role of a developmental helper.
Needless to say, this involves the absolute renun-
ciation of force. The pedagogy of flogging, which is
still widely working its mischief in many parts of the
world, was vehemently opposed by Adler and his
collaborators. It is one of the outstanding achievements of individual psychology that it drew the general public's attention to the deleterious consequences of beatings and punishments in the
educational system. But the disastrous effects of authoritarian education are still not recognized everywhere, and in many places it is precisely the school
that promotes the spirit of punishment and absolute
obedience which has undreamt-of consequences in
the life of an individual as well as in culture.

A nonauthoritarian school must also liberate the
child from the pressure of grades and report cards,
which hang over many children like a heavy cloud.
As soon as the school system is freed from the prin-

ciple of ambition and achievement which stems from economic competition, it is logical to support the slow learners instead of dropping them. The individual psychological class community is encouraged to admit the "poor pupil" to its team. In this community the more competent student learns to feel responsible for the weaker student and to give him his aid. Children who would have to be kept back are supported by their schoolmates or by increased efforts on the part of the teacher until, by virtue of their willingness to practice and teach themselves, these children are able to keep up with the class. Since individual psychology, apart from organic illnesses, does not believe in lack of talent, it arouses in the educator that boundless optimism which makes his optimistic predictions come true. Actions and reality have shown—experimentally, as it were— that by applying the principles of individual psychology it was possible to transform "untalented" into talented pupils. This can be done if the teacher knows how to overcome a pupil's discouragement and to induce him to undertake patient practice.

All this is possible only if the teacher possesses psychological knowledge and thus is in a position to have a profound understanding of his pupils' superficial symptoms. A child's incompetence in one or more subjects, as well as his lack of discipline or talent, always have a deeper meaning, which can be elucidated only on the basis of his *life situation*. If a teacher wishes to clarify this, he must be able to carry on a psychological conversation with the pupil and usually also with his parents. Spiel has published fine examples of this which describe the teacher as the *"Régisseur* [stage manager] of the class community." But this technique of conversation and guidance is not merely a rational method;

it is dependent on the well-developed and psychologically trained personality of the teacher. For this
reason individual psychology has demanded that
every pedagogue acquire self-knowledge and have
himself reeducated by means of a *character analysis*
so that he may be equal to his task. This would enable him not only to transcend any flaws in his personal development (which can include all sorts of
psychological ills) but also to acquire the tools for
an early diagnosis of psychological maldevelopments in children, as well as the capacity to have a
beneficial influence on them. Only if the teacher is
himself a sound, balanced, and psychologically understanding person will he be able to approach children as a friend and model and impart to them the
social feeling that has been awakened in him.

Individual psychology also advocates a *moral-
ization* of the schools by asking them to provide
training in humanistic ethics through their spirit and
the selection of what is taught. In this spirit, the
glorification of war, nationalism, and hero worship
belong to the past as much as does the principle of
an ambitious competitive struggle. Through the
presentation of real cultural achievements and the
realization of an educational community based on
the principle of mutual aid, the emotional life of the
pupils should be steered in a direction that makes
them pioneers of progress and cultural development. Thus, Adler's *Understanding Human Nature*
presents, after a discussion of human nature, the
postulate of a *social school*, individual psychology's
best hope for the advancement of civilization and
society.

6

Individual Psychological Characterology

Theory of Character

More than the other schools of depth psychology, individual psychology strives for an understanding of character, which it regards as the foundation of all psychological reactions. It defines character not as a reaction formation to a hypothetical drive constitution but as an attitude of an individual, as the way in which he copes with life. According to Adler, character is a social concept related to the life-style and *Gangart* of a person, which always signify an attitude toward his fellowmen. Through his character traits a person develops guidelines by means of which he can make his way through life, with every character trait containing a mixture of striving for superiority and social interest. The *meaning* of a character lies in the goal for which an individual strives. All character traits are permeated by a person's secret law of movement, which he formulates on the basis of his experiences in early childhood and which he carries over into all his relationships as an unconscious leitmotif.

Within the framework of these views there is, of course, no place for an inherited character structure. Adler sees character not as something determined but as a free creation of the child. The influences of the body (*constitution*) and of the

environment must not be regarded as binding, although a child's sense of life can derive strong impulses (*enticements*) from them.

The transmission of character is an age-old article of faith of prescientific thinking. Vague cor-
respondences between parents and children have
kept feeding this prejudice, and the fact that the
parents' characters exert a constant formative and
determining influence on the growing child was
overlooked. Since the parents constitute the child's
most important environment, he must inevitably at-
tune his psychological development to their character structure, and in addition children adopt many
things from grown-ups through imitation. By listening, borrowing, and imitating the child strives to
become like his parents, whom he perceives as exemplary. Their bigness and complete authority become the measure of the child's own personality
ideal from which he later wrests the character traits
that are meaningful for him.

According to Adler, the character which the
child creates more or less freely as early as the first
years of his life on the basis of his experiences (for
which body structure, position in the sibling order,
educational influences, and economic and social
realities furnish the material) definitely falls within
the coordinate system of striving for power and social interest. All the active forces in the child must
be included in his attitude toward social living. In
view of the social rootedness of a human being, neutral psychological stirrings are unthinkable. Since
an individual must make his way among his fellow
human beings to an actualization of his self and his
worth, each of these stirrings will express the opinion that he harbors of himself and his human tasks.

In this sense individual psychology regards
every expressive movement, be it mimicry, ges-

tures, language, or behavior, as a sign of the deeper structure of a person's character. To the interpretive skill of depth psychology these fleeting phenomena reveal themselves as signposts that indicate the direction a person plans to take. The more constant character traits permanently secure this direction by giving all human relationships or partnerships a specific course which is in keeping with unconscious expectations or apprehensions. This makes these character traits the strongest safeguards of the personality, and they help a person to find in the tangle of human circumstances a "fixed point within himself" from which principles may be formulated that are fictitious but seem familiar. These behavior patterns, which are called *character*, are by their nature changeable and rectifiable. Having been derived from childhood impressions through arbitrary abstraction, they can be subjected to a radical transformation through systematic self-knowledge, achievable through psychotherapy.

According to Adler, the classic theory of temperament also contains misunderstood character traits which must be traced not to bodily factors, as in the medieval concept of the four humors, but to a person's attitude toward life. The anger of the choleric individual is an aggressive character trait which aims at self-assertion in difficult situations, social interest being excluded. The gloominess of the melancholic person is a passive but also aggressive complaint against the environment, which does not satisfy his demands and expectations. The slothfulness of the phlegmatic person, finally, often contains a rejection of the tasks of social living, which a person can easily evade by referring to his temperament, which seems "given". To Adler the healthiest type seemed to be the sanguine individual, and one has to think of such individuals as persons who are ready to give pleasure to others and who contribute their share to the general welfare with energy and *joie de vivre*. Optimism evidently is a gift of life to those who feel as members of the community and face the world not just as takers and receivers but also as *givers*.

In interpreting character as a response of the child to his environment and educative influences, Adler took a step toward a *psychology of position*, which does recognize innate *dispositions* but gives an individual a chance to make creative use of them. In another context he spoke of his psychology of *use* in place of the psychology of *possession*. He said that what a person has been given is not as important as what he makes of it. If a person has drawn bad conclusions from bad childhood experiences, it should not be concluded that he must now be tied to his childhood errors forever; such a person can be helped to change provided one heeds this rule of Adler's: "For us a person's character never is the basis for a moral judgment but for a social understanding of the way this person affects his environment and what his connection with it is."

Character Traits of an Aggressive Nature

From the foregoing presentation it follows that character traits must be evaluated according to the amount of social interest and striving for superiority they contain. Power and superiority can be attained in an active or a passive way. Adler endeavored to fashion a characterology that would do justice to the purposiveness of a person's emotional life and his social rootedness. In the subtle analysis of such psychological attitudes he proved to be a great connoisseur of the psyche who knew how to reconstruct the psychological totality from a detail. His descriptions of character traits equal those of the famed moralists and deserve pride of place in a scientific understanding of human nature.

According to Adler, *ambition* and *vanity* are typical and direct manifestations of the human striving for power. Since this runs counter to social interest, it seldom declares itself openly and undisguisedly but usually hides behind the mask of a sense of community, so as to strive for its egotistical goals all the more unrestrainedly. Both qualities, however, bring a combative element into life, destroy all unaffectedness, and make it impossible for the person afflicted with them to become a good fellowman and fellow player. Adler rightly pointed out that the social atmosphere of the modern world promotes the development of aggressive and asocial character traits. The isolation of one person from another and the economic principle of "war of everyone against everyone" throw an individual upon his own resources, so that personal preeminence seems more important to him than the advancement of the community as a whole. Under this cultural compulsion almost everyone develops a tendency to seem to be more than he is, or at any rate to emphasize his superiority to others over his actual achievement. The exaggerated individualism of our age caricatures itself in the ambition and vanity of individuals who can maintain their self-assessment only if they are "more than the others." Such a basic attitude necessarily leads to alienation from one's fellowmen. A person who is vain and ambitious will inevitably be overly sensitive and insecure as well, and this oversensitivity and insecurity will manifest themselves especially if life does not meet his demands. A neurosis often is the refuge of an ambitious person whose egocentric goals have been wrecked by reality.

Obstinacy, faultfinding, and a tendency to de-
precate are qualities that grow on the soil of ambition and vanity and express a belligerent mentality in various forms. Adler calls the striving to be
godlike, which a psychotic occasionally manifests
verbally, as the ultimate aim of neurotic ambition.
In his delusion the psychotic expresses the secret
desires of all mentally ill people when he acts as
though he were all-powerful— God, an emperor, or
a cabinet minister. Individual psychology confirms
the old insight of La Rochefoucauld that all psychological stirrings contain a bit of self-love, which
is kept concealed by a healthy individual and even
in a mentally ill person is revealed only by a subtle
interpretation.

Another direct and aggressive character trait is
jealousy. As in the case of ambition and vanity,
Adler regarded this trait as an asocial compensation
for a child's feeling of inferiority, involving material
of childhood experiences that enters adult life uncomprehended. Children who are, or believe they
are, disadvantaged develop feelings of jealousy
early on; those who have been pushed out of their
privileged position by a younger sibling are particularly susceptible to jealousy. This is usually coupled with envy and hostility. A pronounced jealousy
is a childhood neurosis, even though it is usually
disregarded by the educators or merely kept in
check through admonition and rebuke. Thus it happens that a childhood neurosis grows into an adult
neurosis, and a type of person develops who, with
his belligerent and mistrustful mentality, is insuf-
ficiently prepared for community living. This manifests itself particularly in love relationships: a jeal-
ous person would like to take possession of the
partner and dictate to him or her through jealousy
what he or she may or may not do. That this kind

of dominance is detrimental to the couple's life together can easily be demonstrated.

Envy and *avarice* complete the picture of aggressiveness which leaves all fellowmen behind as
it strives for the larger-than-life goal of power. Envy,
too, is merely a continuation of a child's sense of
deprivation, which can take root in childhood under
various conditions. The general framework for this
universally human character trait is furnished by the
actual straits of the majority of mankind, and the
envy of the have-nots will be eliminated only when
these people have been given better living conditions that are more suitable for human beings. In
childhood it is primarily the parents' love for which
one child, rightly or wrongly, envies another child.
A sense of deprivation of this type can degenerate
into a greedy desire to have everything, which never
gives the person concerned any peace. Either he is
consumed with unfruitful jealousy (which occasionally can even be recognized from his gestures and
postures) or he avariciously amasses possessions
which let him savor the thrill of power beyond material security. Money as the equivalent of power
gains a central importance in life, and in this sense
the capitalistic cult of wealth and moneymaking as
a criterion for human perfection is very seductive.

In all the above-mentioned qualities there is a
trace of *hatred*, without which an aggressive and
egotistical mind set can hardly be imagined. Adler
repeatedly emphasized that our civilization promotes the development of feelings of hate. Such features as its nationalistic, religious, and racist ideologies, the glorification of war and militarism, and
class differences are germ cells of hostility which
the psyche of an individual can hardly escape. The
criminal who raises misanthropy to the status of a
watchword and seeks to exploit the community in

his way acts no differently from those who sin against the community spirit on a far greater scale under the cloak of legality. The epidemics of hatred which afflict the mass psyche from time to time manifest in frightening fashion our deficient cultural development, in which the common welfare is continually sacrificed to the delusion of dominance by an individual or a clique.

Character Traits of a Nonaggressive Nature

The direct path to the attainment of power frequently turns out to be difficult because the environment reacts to hostile characters with rejection or hostility. Thus in many cases there are reverses which encourage the individual concerned, usually as early as his childhood, to pursue his goal of self-aggrandizement indirectly. The striving for superiority is here subject to a change of form which completely alters it outwardly but leaves its core untouched. It was Adler's astute intuition that discovered the secret aggression behind seemingly passive characteristics. One not only can attack or exploit the community openly but also can strive to overcome others in a thousand devious ways. Aggression may be replaced, for example, by hostile isolation or deficient contributions, and even if the person who acts in this way does not hurt anyone else, his behavior means an impairment of a community that is dependent on social relationships and cooperation.

Seclusiveness results from an aggressive drive that has become passive and led to abandonment of communal ties. There are people who put a certain distance between themselves and others through their demeanor, through the way they talk or listen. This standoffishness contains elements of ambition.

One finds this tendency in more or less marked form in almost all neurotics; they tend to withdraw to a smaller sphere of life in order to be able to survey it, dominate it, or agitate it all the more assuredly. Adler named the *pathos of distance*, as rightly described by Nietzsche for the artist, as a characteristic of every psychogenic illness. In the social realm isolation also plays an important role, as evidenced by the self-exaltation of classes or social strata.

It seems more difficult to demonstrate the aggressive connections in *anxiety*. But fearfulness invariably is also a loosening of social connections and always appears where interest in, and concern for, the environment have not been sufficiently developed. Usually this involves a type of person who, in Adler's words, "has not felt at home on earth and among his fellowmen." This gives rise to a person's tendency to evade difficulties, think of himself more than of others, and always have retreat in mind, as it were— a situation that can be made permanent by the precipitation of an anxiety affect. Thus anxiety becomes a tactic of delay; concern with its avoidance impedes all useful activities, and hence the entire rhythm of life stagnates. The result is that while nothing happens to the anxiety-ridden person, he does not accomplish anything worthwhile either. From the anxiety of children one can learn that the anxiety affect also contains a gesture of soliciting help, a signal to the environment which the anxious person hopes will bring him protection and security. It is the same way with an adult's anxiety; it always keeps the environment on the alert and accordingly becomes a means of dominating it passively. Hence anxiety, shyness, or timidity can be eliminated only by moderating one's demands on life. From the viewpoint of individual psychology, this means encouragement and arousal of the social interest that has been stifled in childhood, the social interest that can induce a person to abandon his ego-centric aloofness from the problems of life.

The passive character traits are *evasive tendencies* which give the impression that those concerned are looking for pretexts or excuses. A person preserves a vestige of importance if, by referring to some inhibitions or insecurities, he can represent himself as a sufferer; this follows the childhood pattern that allowed him to receive more than his share of mother love when he took sick or felt pain. But Adler believes that the constant search for extenuating circumstances is hardly designed to permit a proper life-style. Anyone who shirks his tasks in life cheats himself out of his self-actualization.

According to Adler, *uncontrolled bodily functions* are also an expression of a disturbed general disposition and manifest an aloofness from the required integration into the community. In childhood this appears as unmannerliness of all kinds, be it in the form of dirtiness, nail bitting, or deficient table manners. These modes of behavior, which pose a great problem to the educators, involve more than regrettable bad habits, which is the way they are perceived by the adult fighting them; here the child's total psychological development has been arrested and the symptoms cannot be cured until the whole child is put back on the right track.

Bed-wetting and *stuttering*, etc. also belong in this context, and individual psychology, which always emphasizes the social sense of a symptom, reveals it as a disguised aggression against the environment which is denied integration through the child's disturbed function. Those familiar with these phenomena will not be surprised if alongside such character traits we also find intensified feel-

ings of inferiority, negativism in numerous varia-
tions, and covert or overt pessimism.

In pithy characterizations Adler drew portraits
of schoolboylike, pedantic, and submissive persons
who also employ passive means in their fight against
the community. Psychological analysis also reveals
"sad sacks" and "schlemiels," persons who seem to
be victims of bad luck, as the secret captains of their
fate who need some form of arranged affliction for
their antisocial goals or ideals. *Religiosity*, too, can
be such a "passive way to heaven." The self-re-
proaches of a religious person, his contrite sin-con-
sciousness, and his lament about the damnability of
conditions on earth are hardly designed to put him
in the mood for love and social cooperation. As a
result, a person who is excessively worried about
the salvation of his own soul in heaven can only be
of limited usefulness for the earthly welfare of his
fellowmen.

The Neurotic Character

Adler was the first to furnish a fundamental clarification of the phenomenon of the neurotic character, and he did so in his book *Über den nervösen
Charakter* (1912; *The Neurotic Constitution*, 1926).
With this work characterology became a basic aid
of psychotherapy. In detailed comments today considered classic, Adler drew a portrait of the neurotic
psyche, the finer structure of which had been disregarded by the drive novels of psychoanalysis.

In the neurotic character all character traits of
normality reappear. In the realm of neuroticism
there is nothing that could not also be encountered
in a healthy person. Accordingly, in distinction to
earlier practice one should not speak of *degenera-*

tion and one should draw a clear distinction between *healthy* and *neurotic*. Transitions in psychological life are fluid, and a decision as to when and
where a neurosis begins is a matter of emphasis.

In this book, following an appreciation of older
contributions (for example, those of Janet, Breuer-
Freud, and Kräpelin) Adler launches into a comprehensive description of the neurotic psyche
which is unsurpassed to this day. In the neurotic
character he encounters the all-powerful feeling of
inferiority, which he had stressed as decisive for any
psychological development, in intensified form. It
is as though such people were affected by a feeling
of their inadequacy more persistently than other
people, as though they were so mesmerized by their
weakness and helplessness that one cannot help but
speak of an *inferiority complex*. The corresponding
striving for superiority, in its aggressive or nonaggressive form as described above, is also of excessive dimensions and leads to formation of a character in which overweening *ambition* and
oversensitivity appear prominently.

In such a development social interest is deficient, and Adler finds that every neurotic in all his
character traits expects increased hostility on the
part of his environment. This basic feeling, which
derives from specific childhood experiences, gives
rise to *caution* and a *hesitant attitude*— attempts
to face life's dangers with a greater safety factor, as
it were. Hesitation and faintheartedness as a rule
develop into *timidity*, which almost invariably is a
trait of the neurotic character, although it often takes
skilled psychological observation to recognize the
neurotic's anxiety behind his feigned indifference,
contempt, or disdain for that which he fears.

Since, according to Adler, almost all neurotic
persons come from a pampering childhood milieu,

they frequently also have a *need to lean on some-body*, and thereby are unconsciously striving to create an existential situation after the pattern of the pampering situation of childhood. In this sense, all neurotic weakness is aimed at someone in the neurotic's environment, who is thereby to be spurred on to increase his help and contribution. Like all character traits, the neurotic character has a social meaning and is invariably also an appeal to the environment, which is supposed to be considerate and perhaps let itself be dominated.

The intensified feeling of inferiority is of necessity related to a whipped-up striving for power that can utilize forms of expression and realizations of all kinds. All these manifestations, which stem from a low self-assessment, in the final analysis aim at a larger-than-life personality ideal, which Adler summed up as *godlikeness*. On this plane, which a deluded person sometimes verbalizes, there are also more modest goals, such as power, wealth, knowledge, beauty, honor, and pleasure, which a neurotic compulsively dreams of or strives for. Realistic striving is the rare case of a successful compensation for the original inferiority. When the courage to achieve, and to overcome resistance, has not been developed because the social interest has been stifled at an early age, the neurotic contents himself with dreaming and a *will to semblance*, which in the face of life's real problems swerves onto sidetracks and, so to speak, fights the battles of life in an imaginary theater of war.

Other features of the neurotic character are passivity, vacillation, and doubting; in these the *safe-guarding tendency* is also paramount. In hypochondria this tendency affects the bodily activities, which seem threatened by illness everywhere. In pessimism, fate appears as a hostile power that urges caution and readiness for defense. In superstition, finally, security is striven for through pointless reflections, rituals, and prayers which serve the secret intention of tracking down the higher powers and stopping their activities.

Miserable childhood conditions, which hardly ever are characterized by genuine friendship and benevolence toward the child, give rise to the neurotic's tendency to maintain his mind-set through *willfulness* and *obstinacy* and to escape outside influences. The *fighting position* acquired at an early age is frequently carried over into situations that are totally unsuited to it. According to Adler, a neurotic's relationship with the opposite sex is always strained. Under the influence of a patriarchal culture that proceeds from the inferiority of women as a biblical dogma, the neurotic psyche develops an ideal of perfection that has typically masculine features. Hence Adler believes that every neurotic character also harbors the so-called *masculine protest*, which can perhaps be expressed by the statement: I want to be a real man. The goal of being on top, of being male, is contained in every neurotic mentality, usually in hidden form; it becomes apparent in thousands of variants but always as an ideal which the person involved hopes will help him overcome his often exaggerated feeling of inferiority.

Adler's description of the neurotic character is the bridge between normal and abnormal psychology. It is also a guide to the practical understanding of human nature, since all the traits that he described occur not only in psychopathology but also in everyday life. In psychotherapy, finally, it is an indispensable instrumentality for a more profound understanding and for the influencing of nervous and neurotic patients, whose fear of life and un-

worldly goals can be eliminated only by an education for fellowship in the spirit of individual psychology. As social feeling becomes stronger, so does
awareness of reality. As a result, compulsive, neurotic character traits can be replaced by a more flexible adaptation to reality in which the entire life-
style becomes less constrained and more creative.

7

Individual Psychological Psychopathology

Theory of Neurosis

The presentation of the neurotic character already contains the outline of individual psychology's theory of neurosis. Neurosis always grows on the soil of a neurotic character; it is its logical continuation and elaboration under worsened psychological conditions. If an inwardly insecure person who lives with inordinate ambition and egocentric orientation finds himself in greater straits, he tends toward retreat, and in an extreme case these movements can take the form of a neurosis. This is an attitude in which despondency and the need for prestige predominate. What makes it a mental illness is that it gravely impairs a person's ability to live and work.

Neurotic symptoms can be understood only within the context of the personality as a whole; an isolated approach cannot reveal their meaning. Only if one knows with what feelings and opinions a person lives, what degree of courage and social interest he has acquired in earlier life, and where his specific anxieties and apprehensions lie can one understand why he fails in a particular situation, as one may in a test, and undertakes a flight into neurosis. Without deliberate intent a person who feels unable to cope with given circumstances can let the life movements which he has practiced since his childhood develop into a neurosis if this seems necessary to him for the protection of his self-esteem in the face of threatening defeats.

Neurosis is thus a manifestation of existential anxiety and pessimism which compel an individual burdened by unfortunate childhood influences (Adler particularly emphasizes pampering) and beset by overestimated difficulties to adopt a resigned attitude toward life. The inadequacy of the rigid and unworldly dispositions acquired in childhood is manifested by the tasks of life, which are always social in nature and require a well-developed social interest for their satisfactory accomplishment. The emotional shock attendant upon this jars the entire psychophysical organism. As a sign of this acute existential insecurity, *anxiety* gains preponderance and can lead to all kinds of psychological and physical disturbances. Neurosis begins where the standstill of the life movement resulting from anxiety is fixed, where the symptoms usurp the predominant interest of consciousness and severely restrict the afflicted person's sphere of action. In this sense Adler views neurosis as a "declaration of war on life," which involves the opening of a "secondary theater of war" whose care keeps the major front of reality away and decreases the danger that the person's own inadequacy will become manifest.

This interpretation of neurosis has a telic orientation as it permits recognition of the goal and purpose which the peculiar world of neurotic symptoms is supposed to serve. It also makes it clear that the nervous malady creates a comforting distance from life and constitutes a kind of safeguard which the patient feels he needs in accordance with his experiences. Adler even spoke of the "neurotic arrangement." Neurosis surely is not something that happens to a patient who remains passive but rather his way of coping with life, his attempt at compensation through intensified feelings of inferiority. The fact that this involves an exploitation of the social interest of the environment, which is compelled to be considerate of the mental patient, only confirms that the neurosis originates in the world of the pampered child, who believes that his life plan can be secured only if he makes demands on others. Thwarted ambition and the fear of making decisions compel a person to adopt a hesitant and timid, neurotic living technique, and this technique would make sense if life were as hostile and its tasks as insoluble as the neurotic sees them from the perspective of his childhood pattern. The more anxiety-ridden a person's psyche is, the more inflexibly and schematically he must live. A neurotic fails because of the rigidity of his reactions and because of his excessive safety factor, which alienates him from life.

The Adlerian theory leaves no room for doubt that virtually all neuroses derive from childhood disorders. The constancy of the life-style is evidence that the later neurotic must already have been difficult as a child. Those childhood disorders which are usually misunderstood by educators as ill will on the part of the child (such as anxiety, bedwetting, stuttering, nail biting, vomiting, lack of appetite, bad temper, and laziness) have already reached the stage of *childhood neuroses*, which the adult environment combats fruitlessly with inappropriate means. Consequently, unless psychological measures are helpfully employed in childhood, it is logical that sooner or later the difficult child will turn into a neurotic adult. When a child leaves the nursery and reaches the real front of life, an imperfect preparation brings about an inability to solve the problems of human existence, and in the face of more severe conflicts a fully formed neurosis beckons.

As we have already mentioned, only an uninformed observer can speak of a breakdown being like a bolt from the blue. It is equally naive to blame overwork, the vegetative nervous system, endocrine glands, or the like. An informed person always realizes that such people have tended toward their catastrophe from childhood on in that their character traits and goal images have made them misfits in life, in that they have shirked their tasks and fled from decisions they can no longer evade with a gesture of begging for help, as it were, and with demonstrated inadequacy. Their impaired self-confidence causes mental illness as a way out from the claims of a world that demands cooperation and social living.

Adler did not think it was a good idea to draw a sharp distinction between one form of neurosis and another. He believed in the *unity of neuroses* as a form of faulty life-style, of which there are innumerable individual variants. A listing of types often buries the uniqueness of each case in a general schematic representation. There is no such thing as *the* compulsion neurosis, just as there are no anxiety neuroses, hysterias, or other types that can be clearly labeled. And yet some elements of the traditional clinical patterns can be preserved if these are carefully supported with individual psychological diagnoses. According to Adler, all neuroses are within the sphere of influence of anxiety, and anxiety constitutes the dramatic manifestation of the underlying feeling of inferiority. The neurotic symptoms are an expression of, and defense against, anxiety. It depends on a person's history and his psychophysical condition what organs or psychological forms of expression the inferiority complex will employ to start compensatory attempts, of which neurosis is a special instance.

An *anxiety neurosis* is a manifestation of infe-riority feelings and anxiety in the emotional realm, and it appears in persons in whom the emotional sphere seems to have been paramount since child-hood. If one remembers to what extent a child's anx-iety leads to increased help from his concerned en-vironment, the *purpose* of the anxiety symptom, be it fear of open places or some other kind of phobia, immediately becomes apparent: it is a person's ap-peal to the environment not to leave him all alone, not to bother him, to treat him with indulgence, and the like. Exemption from exertion and obligations is on the same level; given the close connection be-tween the anxiety affect and the vegetative nervous system, physical symptoms such as headache, fa-tigue, insomnia, or palpitations can be easily pro-duced or they can be retained if they result from a particular constitution or susceptibility.

Hysteria, the origin and first cause of neurosis research, was frequently traced back to repression in the sexual sphere. According to the findings of individual psychology, the sexual element is of sec-ondary importance here as well. The characteristic thing about the hysterias is the striking and dramatic manifestation of helplessness, a person's theatrical drawing of attention to himself; here, too, the affects dominate the scene. The crude physical manifes-tations, such as paralysis, fainting spells, and loss of speech, are in the realm of a training whose secret watchword (and one that is usually uncompre-hended by the patient) is to make an impression through a demonstration of weakness. This basic feature has often caused people to suspect that hys-teria is simulated, and wrongly so, since it is an obvious fright reaction in which a person who feels helpless rules through weakness. Precisely this last-named formula explains why this illness used to be regarded as the domain of *women*, for their position in cultural history actually permitted no other dominant position in the past.

Compulsion neurosis is, in Adler's view, characterized by the predominance of the intellectual sphere. Obsessive thoughts and compulsive impulses are also barriers against anxiety, which expresses itself again and again—for example, when compulsive acts are suppressed. This form of neurosis generally develops in persons subjected to a strict and faultfinding education, a childhood atmosphere in which hate and suppressed rage are stored up in the child. The generally unfeeling environment promotes the development of pedantry, waywardness, and faintheartedness. Defiance against the compulsion of life is also aroused, and it develops the countercompulsion of neurotic impulses as a weapon, as it were. Ceremonies and the claptrap of formulas become a means of wasting time; these are quite similar to the religious type of behavior and are also related to a child's belief in magic, a belief cultivated also by religion. According to Adler, compulsive washing, obsessive ideas, or other forms of compulsion give rise to the picture of a "busy idleness," which develops into unworldliness and sometimes is closely related to schizophrenia.

Neurasthenia, which used to be regarded as a consequence of the alleged vice of masturbation, is probably close to anxiety neurosis. One can get along without this term as well as the other designations if one accepts Adler's doctrine that all neuroses are expressive of a pampered life-style, which fails when a person faces the problems of life with diminished psychological activity and an increased readiness to lean on others. Curing a neurosis is a matter of a person's self-knowledge and an intensified social interest, which at the same time means a reduction of the need for prestige.

Perversions and Criminality

Adler's interpretation of perversion and criminality radically differs from the psychoanalytic theories, which emphasize the fatalistic factor of disposition. In accordance with the theory of the *polymorphous perverse sexuality* of the child, psychoanalysis regards perversion as a child's being arrested in a standard phase of his libidinal development as conditioned by a constitutional preponderance of the partial impulse concerned, as well as by specific traumas which fixate this stage of the drive. A criminal, finally, is said to suffer from an overdeveloped aggressive instinct, which is beyond sublimation, or to be under the influence of an unbearable guilt feeling, which is to be relieved through the commission of a criminal act.

As an alternative to this mythology of drives, Adler states very emphatically that psychic failures are to be traced back not to drive-related illnesses but to a disease of the whole personality. Only attention to the whole permits us to recognize the deeper connections in psychological life. Then, too, it must be taken into account that a person and his environment are ineluctably interwoven. The communal structure of our life gives rise to the tasks of sexual love and cooperation, against which perverts and criminals rebel in desperate protest. Accordingly, an understanding of these variants of human conduct must begin with the recognition that we are dealing with types that have not adjusted to social living and are, in particular, distinguished by a *lack of social interest.*

Here, too, Adler relegates the factor of disposition to the sphere of speculation. Anyone who knows how to make adequate use of the means of psychological analysis need not have recourse to the dubious idea of heredity. Blind fate, which people would like to localize in the genes, is very palpable in the cultural and social conditions. The mendacious sexual morality and the religious prudery which the unnatural philosophy of the past has forced upon children are as much responsible for the enormous incidence of perversions as war, privation, mass misery, and the capitalistic-individualistic ideology are to blame for the ineradicability of crime.

According to Adler, the basic feature of the sexual perversions— such as homosexuality, sadism, masochism, fetishism, and exhibitionism—is the elimination of the loving relationship to the other sex. Because of his childhood impressions and his experiences in later life, the pervert does not feel up to such a relationship. For this reason he rebels against the normal sexual role, which, in accordance with his preparation for life, he fears will bring about a devaluation of his personality. This fact usually remains unconscious, and what comes to the fore is principally a rejection or deprecation of women by means of which the man compensates for his own inferiority feelings. This becomes especially clear in homosexuality, but it also underlies the other perversions. The pervert is always a person who has been excessively burdened in childhood and has acquired a very deep-rooted feeling of inferiority as well as a distorted view of sex and love life. His perversion is an attempt composed of hypersensitivity, irritated striving for superiority, and distrust to keep his distance from the other sex or to attain an imagined superiority to it. It is invariably a matter of an evasive tactic, a pattern adopted in childhood which often seems like their real nature to those concerned because they started their training in that direction in their first years of life.

Criminality is also a way of life in which the capacity for cooperation and social living has remained underdeveloped. Lombroso's concept of the born criminal is a fanciful generalization that must be reduced to the findings of individual psychology. According to these, crime is based on a *Gangart* [gait] and technique of life practiced since childhood which is characterized principally by increased activity and decreased social interest. Criminals are people who have learned as children not to be "co-men" but "counter-men". The conditions, in particular the social ones, which they encountered induced them to regard the world as enemy territory. To the extent that there was activity, this led to a belligerent attitude aimed at the damaging, disadvantaging, and outwitting of the environment.

The viewpoint of individual psychology is confirmed by the fact that numerous criminals were orphaned, illegitimate, unwanted, ugly, or neglected children. In such cases the lack of love in childhood constitutes the prelude to a life in which the inclination toward mutual aid and a social contribution can only have a minor place. In the face of their stunted social interest it should not be surprising that such people succumb to temptation more readily than those who feel integrated into the mainstream of communal life. The former are more likely to interpret a predicament as an invitation to invoke

the law of the jungle and generally live by the precept that only trickery or force can lead to success.

In addition to neglected children, those who
are pampered and made dependent might find
themselves on the road to criminality. This becomes
comprehensible if one is acquainted with the characteristic of constantly taking and desiring in the
emotional life of this type of person. Such a person's
life is based on the use of the contributions of others
for his own benefit without making a useful contribution himself. The pampered child who can extort
everything he desires carries this life-style over into
his adulthood. His aggressive self-assertion within
the framework of his family becomes the prelude to
a future in which triumph and superiority are expected from a struggle against society.

According to Adler, the criminal is a coward
who evades the problems of life and takes refuge in
crime. He is enabled to do so by the erroneous attitude toward life which he has practiced since
childhood and in which the "law of the jungle" has
replaced cooperation. This existential error remains
incorrigible until better and more socially oriented
experiences bring about an inner transformation.
That this happens relatively seldom under present-
day conditions seriously calls into question all institutions that concern themselves with this problem. It is true that reform schools and institutions
for juvenile delinquents or adult criminals are already influenced by the spirit of depth psychology,
but they still fail to meet many demands that are
indispensable for the reeducation of delinquents.

As individual psychology sees it, the task of
society is not to punish a delinquent but to cure him.
The psychological wounds which his family and his
environment have inflicted upon him cannot be

healed by the infamous strict regime of the past. Therapy for crime must primarily consist in an encouragement of the stifled social interest; in addition there should be schooling and vocational training, as well as psychotherapeutic talks aimed at changing the delinquent's life plan. Finally, the crime prophylaxis must start with the education of children, and according to Adler, a school that applies the insights of individual psychology has the greatest chances of diagnosing asocial developments at an early stage and of treating them.

Psychology of Prostitution

Adler's lively social sense was also touched by the problems of prostitution. Prostitution is closely related to the sexual perversions, and like them it requires an individual psychological interpretation. The strange fact that in all human societies there are men and especially women who transform their sexual function into a livelihood deserves the attention of every psychologist. Anyone who desires to obtain deeper insights must, naturally, refrain from any moral presumptuousness. An understanding of prostitution calls for a calm consideration of the facts rather than the moralistic pose of a self-righteous philistine.

For Adler there was no doubt that although society proscribes prostitution, it also participates in its preservation. No one can disregard the fact that sex for sale is an institution promoted by society, an "anal structure" created by it which it feels it cannot do without. The generally accepted view is that prostitution is a sensible supplement to marriage. The fact that it is ineradicable leads many to make gloomy reflections about human nature or becomes the source of generalizations about the power of the sex drive in contrast to the weakness of human reason. Occasionally someone makes the resigned statement that we have to reckon with prostitution as something natural and unalterable.

Individual psychology's contribution to clarifying the problem of prostitution leaves moralistic considerations aside and views the social structure as the real source of prostitution. According to Adler, this phenomenon can appear only in situations in which a woman is regarded as a means of sexual pleasure and an object for satisfying male desire. It is this basic concept of patriarchal civilization that makes prostitution possible. The prejudice of the man's superiority and the woman's inferiority is already implied in the biblical myth of the Fall and other myths, and incidental illustrations of it may be found in the love and sex practices that are degraded into a business because in our civilization a man generally views a woman as an object for sale.

Among those who need prostitution Adler found types of people who displayed many features of the neurotic character described by him. Persons who love to skirt difficulties and seek to garner cheap triumphs in life are more easily drawn into the circle of a prostitute's clients than emotionally better balanced characters. The fear of women, which in a patriarchal climate thrives as much as the underestimation of them (and is similar in nature), is also an impulse toward prostitution, especially for shy, timid, and shabby persons, as well as those who lack social contacts. This also applies to perverts, whose offbeat sexual desires are also born of fear of normal love relationships. Drunkards, characters with a heightened craving for recognition, criminals, and semicriminals are also close to prostitution, not to mention the enormous number of occasional customers who from time to time attempt to heighten their sense of self by enjoying the sexuality of a prostitute. Often this is bound up with an unconscious act of vengeance against a lawful wife, with the husband striving to become superior to her through this eminently "male behavior." Adler also points out that in our social order many marriages are similar to prostitution; here we do not necessarily think of marriages that represent business arrangements, but possibly of a very inferior person's choice of a partner which can be based on emotional premises not unknown to the world of love for sale.

Social critics have often blamed misery and poverty for giving rise to prostitution. There is much truth in this, and today it is the privation of the masses that becomes the inexhaustible source of prostitution. A future society that replaces its moral duplicity with a genuine advancement of the general welfare will undoubtedly make great progress in the combating of prostitution. A more accurate psychological understanding, however, goes beyond pointing a finger at the economic conditions, extremely important as they are. Even among impoverished people there are differences in behavior that require interpretation in the spirit of individual psychology.

The psychology of prostitutes was misunderstood for a long time. Lombroso's concept of the born prostitute is as passé today as his concept of the born criminal, although the notion still haunts some uninformed minds. Objective observation also teaches us that prostitutes are not people "suffused with sensuality." In practicing their profession they are usually frigid, and their tenderness is reserved for their paramours or procurers, not infrequently also for their Lesbian lovers. In their profession they are strictly nonsexy "saleswomen" who in the love for sale relationship at best feign sexual pleasure in

order to give their clients the illusion of their effective masculinity.

This fact provides Adler with the key to an understanding of the psychology of individual prostitutes. Apart from marginal cases of women who
have more or less accidentally drifted into prostitution, the profession is a striking demonstration of
the *masculine protest* which, according to Adler,
affects almost all women in a male culture. Only in
a society that suffers from the cancer of a prejudice
about the inferiority of women is prostitution possible— and indispensable. Only women who are
profoundly convinced of the truth of this prejudice
can sell their bodies for money; only men to whom
male superiority seems desirable and valid are suitable clients of prostitutes. The general sexual
suppression within religious dogmatism then does
its share to devalue and debase sensuality, and so
"uncleanliness" for many becomes a virtual symbol
of, and stimulus to, sexual desire.

The individual misfortune created by this finds
its parallel in deplorable mass phenomena, of which
the spread of venereal diseases is only one detail.
It is understandable that the mendacious campaigns
for the solution of this problem which society keeps
launching are doomed to failure until a basic change
is made in the relationship between the sexes generally.

Prostitutes as well as their pimps are necessary
consequences of our ascetic (antisensual) religion
and patriarchal male society. Only in a civilization
in which a woman smarts under the sting of her alleged inferiority will disadvantaged female types hit
upon the idea of lodging a protest by imitating
men—that is, proceeding in "male" fashion,
wooing, and breaking the barriers of morality— by
revolting, as it were, against a society infested with

the poison of supermanliness. Then even a woman's frigidity becomes a weapon against the man who believes he is superior and is now analogously cheated by the woman who, like him, is striving for superiority.

The picture of prostitution is brought into true focus only if one views love and marriage— coupled with an enduring sexual communion, companionship, and the raising of children— as a task that requires social interest for its accomplishment. In this light all those involved in the problem of prostitution are unmasked as human types that have acquired only a defective social interest under the deficient conditions of our civilization and hence head for the illusionary goals of superiority by devious routes. The proclivity to achieve cheap triumphs in an illusory world is gladly utilized by all those who, like our power-crazed culture, use prestige politics to escape making the contribution to the general welfare that is demanded of them.

Theory of Psychoses

Adler was one of the first to postulate the psychogenic origin of the so-called endogenous psychoses. While Bleuler, Freud, and Jung made the *unknown X* the center of psychosis, although they had already brought to light the possibilities of interpreting the psychotic contents, Adler espoused the unity of neuroses and psychoses, both of which, obeying similar laws, constitute an individual's erroneous response to the problems of life. As early as 1920 Adler's basic idea that every neurosis contains in somewhat exaggerated form every characteristic of a normal psyche was extended by him to schizophrenia, melancholia, paranoia, and manic-depressive psychosis. Closer observation that

avoids the discouraging principle of heredity man-
ages to demonstrate that the psychoses which academic psychiatry designates as incomprehensible
and inaccessible to empathy are definitely accessible to psychological analysis. The individual psychological clarification of a patient's prepsychotic
history is revealing about these specific illnesses,
and it manifests the close relationship between the
neurotic and the psychotic life-styles; the latter ac-
tualizes to an extreme point the striving for godlikeness in an illusory world, a striving that is based
on inferiority feelings and social isolation.

All strange features of a mental illness can be
interpreted meaningfully and purposefully through
individual psychology. The lack of insight into the
illness, already indicated in neurosis, here becomes
an encouragement to go on living with self-decep-
tion and protection from reality. This break with
logic and sound common sense is necessary to im-
plement the flight from the environment. Delusions
of grandeur and of smallness give almost verbal
expression to the inferiority feeling and its fictive
compensatory endeavors. And in all cases it is resignation and hopelessness which, in a kind of symbolic suicide, escape from a reality that has become
unbearable and find refuge in the wishful world of
delusion.

According to Adler, here too an early overburdening through lovelessness, organ inferiorities,
and a faulty education must play the decisive part.
A superficial observer believes he has explained
enough if he can perhaps demonstrate that a schizophrenic patient had a schizophrenic mother. This
immediately leads to the banal assertion that a he-
reditary illness is involved, but this disregards the
fact that severely neurotic or mentally ill mothers
are more certain to damage their children through

their association with them and their demeanor than through the hypothetical inherited material. Like neurosis, psychosis is no mere adversity; it is the life path, the creative achievement of a type of person who is overwhelmed by anxiety, who, because of a hypersensitivity heightened by experiences in early childhood, suffers a breakdown in a seemingly insignificant situation. The frequently described inaccessibility to empathy of this process speaks not so much against its comprehensibility as against the understanding of the interpreters. Depth psychology has amply demonstrated that what is a trifle for one person can constitute the catastrophe of another person's life.

Schizophrenia as the most important of the mental illnesses is described in current depth psychological literature as comprehensible and curable. The works of Sechehaye, Rosen, Binswanger, Benedetti, Sullivan, Federn, and others have unraveled the inextricable tangle of delusion formation to a considerable extent, and it is now possible to read the most offbeat psychotic reactions like an open book. Psychotherapeutic experiments like those of the above-mentioned authors, and also those of Frieda Fromm-Reichmann, have demonstrated that psychosis, too, only represents a response to life's problems, a way of life which in the psychotic's rejection of contacts with his fellowmen barely expresses the patient's remaining capacity for relationships. Only if the psychotherapist can break through the wall of mistrust which such people have put up around themselves, and if by virtue of his social interest he relieves the patient's great depression, will the latter open up to him and return to reality from the caves and other hideouts of his delusion.

Melancholia, too, reveals "pantomimically," as it were, the discouragement that leads the patient to reject contacts and contributions. Self-accusations on the part of the melancholiac are reminiscent of the neurotic's wasting of time, but they also are a means of moral rehabilitation which Adler expressed in the epigrammatic formula: I am noble too. Nietzsche called pangs of conscience "indecent"; he evidently realized that their excess impedes a true recovery. The meaning of depression must be derived from the melancholiac's social relatedness. What he does or does not do is an appeal to the environment to exempt him from making a contribution, as well as a constant accusation which his life-style, on the basis of his childhood impressions, suggests to him as appropriate.

In manic-depressive psychosis Adler encountered the neurotic technique of rushing from despondency to sham efforts and sham victories in caricatured form. Both phases of this illness demonstrate the dialectic of inferiority complex and striving for superiority in a crass stylization. The antisocial component is manifested in depression through such actions as a rejection of contacts or suicide attempts, in mania through presumptuousness, irresponsibility, and possibly damage to objects and persons. Behind the manic cheerfulness and the *machismo* the knowledgeable professional seldom fails to notice the patient's completely shattered self-esteem. Here one can, so to speak, put one's hands on the psychotic "life-lie." In paranoia, too, Adler reencountered these connections in complete form; his comments in *Praxis und Theorie* may be regarded as exemplary.

Adler's therapeutic optimism also foresaw the possibility of psychotherapy in such cases, and he was able to report cases that he succeeded in curing. These case studies also contain the theoretical tools which he supplied for future research. The psychotherapeutic treatment of the psychoses and their interpretation have made copious use of them.

8

Individual Psychological Psychotherapy

Educational Guidance and Therapeutic Pedagogy

Adler was the first and most important promoter of depth psychology in the area of the education of children. Psychoanalysis turned its theories to practical use relatively late. For this its educational pessimism, which attributed far more influence on character formation to the *drive constitution* than to education, may be responsible. In accordance with the highly speculative tendencies of its creator, the psychology of Jung developed into a "psychology of the second half of life," which had no interest in children, since their emotional life offered little scope to search for the nebulous archetypes. Only individual psychology seized the educational opportunities offered by the rich experiential material of psychotherapeutic practice. From the theory of the neuroses Adler and his pupils derived an educational prophylaxis which soon developed into a comprehensive psychological pedagogy. This also made them pioneers in child psychotherapy; their accomplishments in this field are so great that they can hardly be sufficiently appreciated. The ideas of individual psychology have permeated everyday education to such an extent that most people do not realize the origin of their views and insights. Thus

Adler's work for an improved education of children has become common property in the finest sense of the term.

As early as 1913 Adler and his pupils published a collection entitled *Heilen und Bilden* [Healing and educating] which testified to the educational importance of individual psychology. Shortly after World War I Adler created child guidance clinics in Vienna which offered free psychological counseling to parents and children. These clinics later achieved an undreamt-of effectiveness in the English-speaking countries. It is usually forgotten that the principles of this guidance activity were established in the more than twenty individual psychological guidance centers of the city of Vienna that came into being under Adler's aegis. In these centers Adler personally and publicly practiced child psychotherapy and conducted conversations with parents in the presence of his pupils and interested teachers. It was his opinion that psychological maldevelopments should be freely discussed. His conversations with children and parents made an indelible impression on many who experienced them. A report on these may be found in the book *Technik der Individualpsychologie*, which offers readers a chance to become acquainted, on the basis of concrete cases, with Adler's intuition and sensitivity in the grasping of the psychological situation of problem children.

The individual psychological viewpoint that every psychological disturbance arises from unfavorable childhood impressions strongly emphasizes the importance of a psychologically correct education of children. Adler repeatedly stressed that parents usually lack the psychological equipment for their difficult assignment; they set about educating their child in utter ignorance of his psychological condition. Sooner or later this is bound to give rise to great misunderstandings, which lay the foundation for all sorts of maldevelopments. Hence it is a matter of imparting to the parents in purely rational fashion the pedagogical knowledge that will permit them to understand the nature and the reactions of a child's psyche. Pedagogy should be learned like any other profession. In the activities of their local groups, the individual psychologists turned to the parents and teachers and carried on a fruitful educational activity, which, unfortunately, was disrupted by the unfavorable circumstances of the times, such as fascism and war.

But education is more than rational action, since one educates not only through what one does but also through what one is. For this reason the *education of the educators* is an indispensable goal of any psychological influence on pedagogy. Thus the educational guidance of individual psychology always involves a parallel treatment of children and parents, since this is the only road to lasting success.

What are the tasks that face child guidance and therapeutic pedagogy? The parents who consult a psychotherapist are usually beset by problems they cannot solve. Usually, and unfortunately, they do not come until they have, as the saying goes, tried everything. Affection, persuasion, strictness, and harshness have been of no avail; the child and the parents are in a fighting position, and the conflict causes all concerned to suffer to a great or lesser degree.

Individual psychology regards every difficult child neither as bad nor as afflicted with bad dispositions and the like. It is always an *erring and discouraged child* who resists the educational measures of his environment because of the inappropriate attitude of his educators. The behav-

ior of every problem child— be it obstinacy, timidity, bed-wetting, stuttering, failure in school, lying,
stealing, or other undesirable actions or attitudes—
is caused by inferiority feelings, which are compensated for in a socially worthless way. In other
words, the development of the social interest of such
children has been arrested and deadlocked. Hence
the child seeks a path *against* his environment, rebels against it, and indicates with his symptoms that
he does not feel at home in it.

All so-called childhood disorders are actually
childhood neuroses, and unless they are corrected
by psychological intervention they frequently develop into adult neuroses. Usually there is no awareness that a "difficult" child is actually an emotionally ill or irritated child. Every kind of
maladjustment stems from the isolation and helplessness of the child, from an oppressive feeling of
insufficiency that calls forth a disturbance as a response. The indignant or punishing adult overlooks
this connection until individual psychology teaches
him that every childhood defect is the consequence
of adult defects. From this individual psychology
consistently derives its rejection of any punitive and
authoritarian education. Through understanding
and help the errant child must be shown a new path
on which he can transcend his inferiority feelings
by socially acceptable means. Rigid training and
strict discipline only perpetuate abuses that have
already taken root in the child's emotional life.

Child guidance and therapeutic pedagogy must
make the *meaning* of developmental disturbances
clear to both the parents and the child. In this area
a considerate course of action is essential if the situation is to be improved, and one should continue
to be guided by the individual psychological doctrine that all childhood disorders are intended to
draw the attention of the environment to the child.

A discouraged child chooses the methods of obstinacy, anxiety, laziness, and apparent lack of talent in
order to be the center of attention, to be noticed,
and to find a substitute for the affection that seems
unattainable to him. This revolutionary view of individual psychology makes all difficulties of education appear in a new light, teaching gentleness
and kindness even toward a problem child whose
uneducability must be interpreted as a desperate
desire for affection. The senselessness of the traditional behavior of parents, including punishment,
scolding, threats, and mockery, can be made clear
only from this vantage point. Authoritarian measures will never significantly change a child; only
encouragement and the insightful correction of his
attitude toward life can help him progress.

The therapeutic pedagogy of individual psychology, then, consists in informing and training the
parents as well as in encouraging and training the
child. The latter is of great importance for successful
therapy. Children who feel inferior miss significant
opportunities to acquire knowledge and develop
their abilities; if the child's feeling of his own worth
is to be strengthened, the treatment must compensate for these missed opportunities. As soon as the
situation has been explained to the child and to his
parents, he must be taught to offset his inadequacies. The educational optimism of individual psychology and its deep-rooted belief that every person
who has all his faculties can be trained to achieve
a certain competence in all things guide all the endeavors with which Adler's teachings have enriched
the entire field of therapeutic pedagogy.

Psychotherapy

The psychotherapeutic practice of individual
psychology is a logical outgrowth of its theoretical

premises. The aim here is to help the patient or the person seeking counsel to gain a different attitude toward life through self-knowledge. To this end a systematic treatment is initiated in which the personality of the patient is to be recognized and understood.

Unlike Freud, Adler viewed the psychotherapeutic process as an effective interaction between the therapist and the patient. To this day psychoanalysis observes the rule that the analyst should resemble a mirror that can always reflect the patient's psychic conditions in unaltered form. This idea also finds expression in the use of the famous psychoanalytic couch; having the patient lie on a couch and voice his associations without being able to see the psychoanalyst creates the greatest possible distance, and the relationship precludes any closer communication of feelings and thoughts. The fact that the analyst sits and observes the supine analysand without being observed by him gives the analyst a position of superiority. In the couch method the therapist cannot help regarding his patient as an object, and a genuine human encounter is almost impossible because of the different positions of those involved.

To individual psychology, psychotherapy is a free collaboration between the therapist and the patient. They sit opposite each other and carry on the *psychological interview*, with the patient being considered a partner of equal value and with equal rights. The analytic work is regarded as collaboration and teamwork whose purpose is the patient's self-exploration as guided and inspired by the therapist. In contrast to adherents of other psychological schools, the individual psychologist from the beginning counteracts his authority with the patient. As a matter of principle he places himself on the level of human fellowship, and he must make every effort to avoid any authoritarian position, which, according to Adler, is bound to lead to failure. Adler also advised making it plain that the responsibility for a cure lies with the person who is counseled, that the cure is the result of *his* efforts and *his* inner transformation. As a dramatic illustration of this fact he would refer his pupils and patients to the English proverb: You can lead a horse to water, but you can't make him drink.

The structure of individual psychological therapy is a network of education, counseling, and therapy of the patient. One can distinguish among various stages which, to be sure, are separable only in theory and are connected in practice.

The person seeking counsel or the patient who consults a psychotherapist is in trouble or would like to acquire some self-knowledge for professional and personal reasons. He might suffer from certain symptoms or disturbances which he would naturally like to eliminate. He is now supposed to participate in therapeutic treatment which is to enable him to understand himself and to change.

To this end it is, first of all, absolutely necessary to create a *situation of trust* in which the psychological treatment can be accomplished. The therapist explains the meaning and the method of the psychotherapeutic process and places himself at the counseled person's disposal for his self-exploration. He explains to him that they want to clarify the patient's attitude toward life in *free conversations*, that their material will be the life story and the present reactions of the patient, and that these will supply information about the structure of his personality. In order to inspire the counseled person's confidence, the psychologist must do more than master the theoretical tools of his trade; he must himself be

a stable and balanced personality capable of building a strong human relationship with a usually
rather difficult (for example, a hypersensitive, nervous, or distrustful) person. According to Adler, this
task is considerably facilitated if the therapist has
no axe to grind, that is, if he does not abreact any
personal ambitions or sensibilities but keeps aiming
solely at the furtherance of his partner in conversation with companionable benevolence, equable
helpfulness, and an infinite amount of patience. If
the psychotherapist maintains a balanced human attitude, he need not fear that he will encounter the
phenomena of *transference* and *resistance* that psychoanalysis emphasizes. Freud also squeezed the
therapeutic relationship into his libidinal scheme
and tried to conclude from it that the patient is li-
bidinously attached to the therapist and that his repressed material resists becoming conscious. In the
nature of things, the process of self-recognition involves some pain, but a skillful therapist avoids both
the libidinous dependence of his patient and any
affront that is bound to produce reactions of offense
and diminished cooperativeness.

The psychotherapeutic interview revolves
about the patient's psychological processes, his motives, reactions, and reflections. From the patient's
life story and his description of his present situation
a knowledgeable therapist learns a great deal about
the patient's attitude toward his life. The chronic
problems and errors in the life of the person seeking
counsel become apparent relatively fast and come
to the fore when his attitude toward the *three tasks
of life* formulated by Adler is illuminated. From a
person's *line of movement* it is possible to divine
his secret goal to which all diagnostically usable observations point: character traits, expressive phenomena, childhood memories, dreams, and opin-

ions on all problems of life. By correctly interpreting the psychological condition of the person seeking guidance, as well as his history and his personal problems, the therapist influences his patient and lays a fresh foundation for his further psychological development.

Psychotherapy is not an essentially intellectual process, however. The psychological treatment must lead to an *experience* that makes possible an inner transformation and reorientation. This transformation must take place in the relationship between the therapist and the person seeking counsel, that is, it must be stimulated and practiced there. To this end it is necessary to give the patient *encouragement* that helps him overcome his real and imagined inadequacies. According to the principles of individual psychology, discouragement is the cause of all psychological failures. The most varied childhood impressions give rise to altogether individual forms of discouragement, and the real task of therapy is to eliminate these. The feeling of inferiority, as first described by Adler, has as many manifestations as there are people. Only if a therapist can uncover the specific causes and make his patient aware of them will there be a successful cure. To encourage a person is a skill that can be learned through the technique of individual psychology, but only training and the most sensitive fellow feeling can develop it to the degree of subtlety that is required in psychotherapy.

By receiving a realistic picture of himself the patient gains a feeling of responsibility for himself and gets to know his strengths and potentialities. His inner feeling of freedom is heightened and his sense of his own worth is fortified. At the same time he attains to a higher degree of social relatedness as well as a change in his value system. The therapy of individual psychology aims not merely at making a person capable of work and enjoyment; it wants to improve him by initiating a moral development. The therapeutic process is virtually "read off" from the growing social interest. As the psychotherapeutic work makes the patient well, his horizon in thought and action is widened. In addition, he takes a socially more stable route on his way through life, that is, he becomes happier and more productive because of his increased readiness to participate in the life of his fellowmen and of the community.

Group Therapy

Individual psychology has also made significant contributions to the development of group therapy. Shortly after World War I Adler began to introduce group educational guidance and parent training in Vienna. In contrast to the psychoanalytic view that human problems and conflicts must definitely remain within the private sphere, Adler found that an objective discussion in a circle of sympathetic people could exert a particularly beneficial and helpful influence. He viewed this as a means of freeing neurotic persons from their isolation and making the group experience accessible to them. The traditional psychoanalytic duad, psychotherapist and patient, was as far as possible to be supplemented with a larger working group in which the rules of community life could be practiced.

Even on the basis of its theoretical premises, individual psychology has very close relationships with group therapy. Adler's doctrine that man is a *social being* is entirely aimed at an understanding of a person's problems on the basis of his relationship with the groups in which he lives and with which he has to deal every day. The guiding insight here is that the way in which a person meets his Thou and his We is fateful for his mental health or illness. An emotionally ill person is characterized not only by such problems as his anxieties, inner disintegration, inferiority feelings, and inhibitions, but also, and primarily, by the facts that he has not really adjusted to the human groups, that he is a stranger in the world of his fellowmen, and that in his isolation and loneliness he falls prey to severe emotional conflicts.

It is at this point that group therapy can begin. In the spirit of individual psychology it must almost always be preceded or accompanied by individual therapy. In practical terms, on the basis of his diagnoses the psychotherapist puts together a relatively harmonious group of five to ten patients, who need not suffer from similar problems or illnesses. This selection of persons who are to discuss their problems and sorrows must be made with the greatest care. Sometimes, after a few sessions it turns out that one person or another does not quite fit into the group, and then this person is offered an opportunity to join another group. It is quite clear that the purpose for which the group constitutes itself is to help each individual. Thus there is formed a temporary community of people who wish to study their attitudes toward life together. In this study the opinion of the Thou acts as a corrective; the group is to teach the individual how other people are doing, how they judge his attitude and his experiences, and what he can learn from this. Anyone who knows how firmly neurotics believe that they alone have problems such as theirs will understand what emotional and intellectual relief the group experience brings. The impression of an open exchange of thoughts and feelings is frequently almost overwhelming and has an extremely favorable therapeutic effect. But the

therapeutic group is not merely a place for instruction and the observation of others; it should, first
and foremost, be training in fellow feeling. Neurotic
people, who always have a hard time finding their
place in the community, learn in this particularly
protected experiment station the technique of social
living and collaboration, and the other members of
the group enable them to catch up on a bit of family
and social development.

Individual psychology keeps emphasizing that
psychologically troubled people have a great need
for social contact. One should not be deceived by
the outward experience of withdrawal, isolation,
and negativism, since in every nervous disorder,
from neurosis to psychosis, social hunger is extraor-
dinarily accentuated. This desire for human attachments, however, is not matched by any well-developed social interest or the ability to associate with
others. The result is a vicious circle of anxiety and
despondency, which leads to increasing detachment from the environment in the type of person
whom childhood impressions have already made
rather antisocial. A person's experience that he can
freely express his thoughts and feelings in the milieu of the group and that he can always count on
receiving enlightenment and encouragement, even
if his improprieties should cause annoyance, is
likely to increase his readiness to make social contacts considerably. Thus the positive aspects of social living are brought home to an individual, and
group discussions give him an impetus to understand himself better and to develop *more adaptive
behavior patterns*. These develop under the guiding light of cooperation and mutual aid and, thanks
to a greater measure of self-knowledge and understanding of human nature, they constitute strong
equipment for real life. The very experience of the

group exerts a powerful influence on a person's inclination to get well by depriving his personal in-
capacities and inadequacies of their "tragic aura"
and letting everyone see that all people face similar
difficulties in their lives.

The technique of group work is based on free
and informal discussions of a strictly democratic
type. Frequent checks are made to ensure that no
one occupies a permanent position of leadership, as
everyone is to learn to be both a leader and a team
player. This basic rule is observed by the therapist
as well. The emotional demands made upon him
are, of course, of a very special kind. If the therapeutic and developmental processes are to be set in
motion, the therapist must not seize the initiative in
the group in the sense of being a master and leader,
but instead he must assume the role of a catalyst
who facilitates many processes but does not directly participate in them. The group therapist must
possess the great skills of mediating between persons of diverse characters (who usually are difficult,
into the bargain), of radiating courage and optimism,
as it were, and of inspiring, through his interpretation, self-knowledge and an understanding of
human nature. Out of a collection of inwardly isolated people he must build a true *group* without
becoming unduly prominent himself. He must also
see to it that every individual in the group can find
out what he is and what he is capable of becoming.
The task of a group therapist could not be described
any better than Nietzsche did under the title "The
Future of the Physician":

There is no profession that permits such growth as that
of the physician. Nowadays the highest intellectual training of a physician has not been attained [merely] if he is
acquainted with the best and latest methods and knows
how to draw those swift conclusions from effects to causes

for which diagnosticians are famous. He must in addition have a persuasiveness that adapts itself to every individual and gets him to bare his soul to him; a manliness which at first sight dispels despondency, the worm damage of every patient; a diplomat's smoothness in mediating between those who for reasons of health must give joy and those who need joy to get well; the sensitivity of a police officer and a lawyer in understanding the secrets of a soul without betraying them— in short, a good physician now needs the artistic devices and privileges of all other professions. Thus equipped, he is able to become a benefactor to society as a whole through the augmentation of good works as well as intellectual pleasure and fruitfulness, through the prevention of bad thoughts and plans as well as villainies, through the creation of an intellectual-physical aristocracy, through the benevolent abolition of all so-called mental anguish and pangs of conscience. Only then will one be able to say that the "medicine man" becomes a savior, and yet he need not perform any miracles, nor does he need to let himself be crucified.

9

Individual Psychology and Literature

Not only do Adler's teachings prove their value in the interpretation of the healthy or diseased emotional life of flesh-and-blood people, but they can also be applied to the imaginary characters in whom great writers have embodied their intuition of the human and all-too-human. The great writers of world literature have anticipated numerous insights of depth psychology by managing to lend so much genuineness and naturalness to the characters that live and act in their works that one can often find all the problems of human existence depicted in them. Hence works of literature are an important source for psychology, and the more receptive and sensitive their interpreter is, the more abundantly and productively will this source flow. Important authors such as Dante, Cervantes, Shakespeare, Schiller, Goethe, Tolstoy, and Dostoievsky, as well as many literary stars of the second magnitude, have in their novels and plays presented a thousand depictions of human nature, and scientific analysis will hardly ever be able to exhaust their wealth of reality. The inner truthfulness of the figures born of the writer's imagination or his dreams derives from his lively concern with them, and this truthfulness gives the reader the sensation that he is dealing with real persons and not imagined ones. The charm of

the aesthetically attractive and convincing presentation is an additional reason why we are spell-
bound by and feel the greatest admiration for the
immortal works of literature. Depth psychology certainly does not try to *dissect* these creations of the
human intellect if it brings their validity to light by
comparing them with its own theories; its only intention is to convey a deeper understanding and an
appreciation refined by insight. As a small sample
of the literary interpretation of individual psychology, we shall present in the following pages a brief
analysis of the figures of Oedipus, Hamlet, Peer
Gynt, and Raskolnikov.

Oedipus Had No Oedipus Complex*

Freud made the myth of Oedipus the corner-
stone of his psychology and of his interpretation of
religion and civilization. He not only interpreted his
hypothesis that every male child would like to kill
his father and marry his mother into Sophocles' tragedy *Oedipus Rex*, but he also made it the basis of all
research in the fields of mythology, prehistory, and
history. In view of the fact that the present tendency
is away from the Oedipus complex and that even
psychoanalysts are beginning to admit that it is not
a normal stage of a child's development but rather
a childhood neurosis, one may well ask whether the
classical drama actually confirms Freud's interpretation. In point of fact, it can be demonstrated without too much difficulty that Sophocles' Oedipus by
no means suffered from an Oedipus complex. Only
a far-fetched interpretation can impute this kind of
symbolism to the action in the tragedy.

* Cf. E. Fromm, *Märchen, Mythen, Träume* (Zurich, 1957); S.
Lazarsfeld, "Had Oedipus an Oedipus Complex?" in *Essays in
Individual Psychology* (New York 1959).

The plot of *Oedipus Rex* requires an interpretation that differs from the psychoanalytic kind. We
must remember that Oedipus upon birth is exposed
on a mountain top because his parents have been
told by the oracle that he would some day kill his
father and marry his mother. Saved from death by
an act of compassion, Oedipus grows up in the royal
palace at Corinth as an adoptive son, learns of the
dire prophecy concerning him, and leaves Corinth.
On his way to Thebes he kills an old man who has
tried to push him off the road; this is none other
than his father Laius. At Thebes he solves the riddle
of the Sphinx and thus rids the city of that monster.
By way of thanks he is made king, and in connection
with this honor (though without his desiring it) he
is given the widowed queen, who is in fact his
mother, for a wife. The tragedy begins years later,
after the city has been visited by the plague and
Oedipus has learned from the seer Tiresias that he
has brought that misfortune upon the city because
of his parricide and incest. In his despair he blinds
himself, while Jocasta, his spouse and mother, com-
mits suicide. According to Freud, the reason for the
drama's powerful and shocking effect is that his sexual tendency in childhood makes every male spec-
tator a potential Oedipus. It is more reasonable to
believe, however, that it is because the hero,
through no fault of his own and without his knowledge, is involved in entanglements that assume a
superhuman dimension.

It is extremely doubtful whether Oedipus, who
came to Thebes as a young man, sought the fulfillment of his sexual desires in the aging Jocasta.
Overcoming the Sphinx brought him, above all, the
kingship as an enhancement of his dignity and his
worth. The characteristic thing about his distinction
is his precedence over all others, and this is still

audible in the words of the chorus after his fall: "Behold, this is Oedipus who unraveled the exalted riddles and was first in power, whose good fortunes all citizens praised and envied; behold in what a stormy sea of dread misfortune he sank!"

The individual psychological interpretation of the Oedipus drama sees in the moving presentation primarily the problem of the generational conflict, which in the patriarchal society degenerates into a power struggle between son and father. In a world in which fathers are concerned with their position of power their sons become threats to their superiority. Laius thought he could escape this by abandoning his little son, but this very offense against the bonds of family life plunges him into perdition all the more surely. His authoritarian and violent behavior toward Oedipus, a stranger, provokes the latter's own violence. The blow he strikes at the head of Oedipus falls back fatally upon his own.

The conflict between father and son which proves Oedipus' tragic undoing is not produced by sexual rivalry but by the desire for power and authority. If one adds interpretations of the dramas *Oedipus at Colonus* and *Antigone*, which must be regarded as continuations of the tragedy, this impression is deepened and becomes ever more convincing. Oedipus himself does not escape the fate of the "toppled authority" which threatens every father in a civilization one-sidedly oriented toward male superiority. His sons Eteocles and Polyneices refuse him any help and thereby provoke their father's hatred and curses. He loves his daughters all the more, for they do not contest his predominance and as women are immune to any competition for power. About them he says: "From these sisters, girls as they are, I get, as their strength permits, food, a secure shelter, and faithful care, while their brothers chose, instead of their father, the throne, the scepter, and the power in the land. Yet they will not find an ally in me."

That Oedipus did not have in mind marriage to his mother, which is what psychoanalysis desires, can also be seen from the fact that Oedipus regards all this as his calamity and an unfortunate entanglement: "In an evil wedlock I became entangled, unwittingly in an accursed marriage."

The grandiose melody of the power struggle pervades the play and the hearts of the spectators, who enjoy it with fear and pity and aesthetic detachment as a parable of the problems of their own lives. Thus the real substance of the tragedy is nothing else but the solution of the riddle of the Sphinx, which marked the beginning of Oedipus' greatness and his downfall. The substance is *man*, whom the chorus praises with these profound words: "Wonders are many, and none more wondrous than man."

Hamlet the Neurotic

Shakespeare's famous play has inspired a depth psychological interpretation from both psychoanalysis and individual psychology. To the psychoanalysts it was evident that the situation of the Danish prince could be reduced to the general scheme of the Oedipus complex. According to them, the reason why Hamlet found it so hard to avenge his father's death was that as a child he himself had desired to kill his father and marry his mother. The uncle who then accomplished this fulfilled Hamlet's unconscious wish as a surrogate. In line with this, the tragedy of the melancholy prince is intended to express the irreconcilable conflict between the dictates of piety toward his murdered father and his basically satisfied unconscious.

This interpretation seems strained, and it requires more credulity than an objective observer can muster. Such schematisms cannot begin to exhaust Shakespeare's wondrous tragedy. Individual psychology is able to bring out different aspects of this masterpiece, aspects which in our estimation are more profound.

The character of the hero is the core and the substance of the entire play. Shakespeare's understanding of human nature proves unsurpassable here. Psychological insight should be able to reproduce the consistency and persuasiveness with which Shakespeare has endowed his title character by deducing from Hamlet's life-style his line of movement in response to what evidently is an extremely serious problem for him.

The task of avenging his father devolves upon him at the very beginning of the play, when his father appears to him as a ghost and names his uncle and his mother as the murderers. Hamlet is ready to avenge his father, but he presents a strange picture of indecision and incaution, an extreme hesitating attitude reminiscent of the neurotic character described by Adler. Goethe, too, seems to have had a similar interpretation in mind when he wrote in his well-known characterization of Hamlet: "A fine, pure, and moral character, but lacking the nervous strength that makes a hero. Every duty is sacred to him, but this one seems too hard for him."

Why does Hamlet lack nervous strength? The modern term for this would be *neurosis*, but the clues for such a diagnosis should not be chosen too lightly. Also, one might keep in mind Adler's reminder that it certainly is hard to kill a person, even if he is the murderer of one's father. Only a holistic evaluation of Hamlet's nature can afford us an insight into his character and thus into his fate.

This character is a strange mixture of reserve and imprudence. With such a momentous resolve in his heart, Hamlet fritters away his time with trivial things and attracts everyone's attention at a time when he ought to be cautious. He makes lengthy reflections which, as with all neurotics, come to a head in the formulation "To be, or not to be, that is the question," but he forgets to act. He distrusts everyone, and shortly thereafter he offends people with his inappropriate frankness. He is long on making plans but short on action: "O God! I could be bounded in a nutshell, and count myself a king of infinite space, were it not that I have bad dreams."

Instead of courageous deeds there are fits of depression, in which Hamlet accuses man and the world. His strength lies in philosophizing: "What a piece of work is man! how noble in reason! how infinite in faculty! in form and moving, how express and admirable! in action how like an angel! in apprehension how like a god! the beauty of the world! the paragon of animals! And yet, to me, what is this quintessence of dust? Man delights not me; no, not woman neither, though by your smiling you seem to say so."

This last remark leads to his relationship with Ophelia, who is driven to madness by his murdering of her father and by the way he treats her. His attitude toward her is a neurotic blend of love and hate which fluctuates between self-accusation and condemnation of the entire female sex. He advises her to trust no man and in the same breath calls himself proud, revengeful, ambitious— and virtuous. The entire mocking-ironic train of thought culminates in this exclamation: "What should such fellows as I do crawling between heaven and earth?" Later, when he cannot pluck up the courage to kill his uncle, this self-criticism and self-condemnation find expression in these electrifying words:

O, what a rogue and peasant slave am I! . . .
Yet I, a dull and muddy-mettled rascal, peak
Like John-a-dreams, unpregnant of my cause,
And can say nothing . . .
Am I a coward?
Who calls me villain? breaks my pate across?
Plucks off my beard, and blows it in my face?
Tweaks me by the nose, gives me the lie i' th' throat,
As deep as to the lungs? Who does me this?
Ha, 'swounds, I should take it; for it cannot be
But I am pigeon-livered, and lack gall
To make oppression bitter . . .

[Act II, Scene 2]

Talking, thinking, dreaming: there lies Hamlet's sphere, which stops close to the border of a world that demands deeds. Through a tricky theatrical performance which mimes the murder of his father he convinces himself— needlessly— once more that his uncle, made completely distraught by the play, is guilty. But a bit later, when he finds the uncle absorbed in prayer, he does not kill him, because he fears that his uncle will then not go to hell. Thus he misses his chance, but he does murder the innocent, loquacious Polonius, who is eavesdropping behind a curtain. This faintheartedness in the face of reality is succeeded by a violent rush to perform a blind deed, which of necessity misses the desired mark.

"Frailty, thy name is woman." In his heart of hearts Hamlet feels that he is not man enough for his deed. He is too deeply convinced of the decrepitude of earthly things to muster the courage to act. The reality in which he does not feel at home is devalued for him in characteristic fashion when he goes to the graveyard and picks up a skull. He says to his friend Horatio:

Dost thou think Alexander look'd a' this fashion i' th'
earth?. . . And smelt so? pah! . . . Alexander died, Alexander was buried, Alexander returneth to dust, the dust
is earth, of earth we make loam, and why of that loam
whereto he was converted might they not stop a beer bar-
rel?

> Imperious Caesar, dead and turn'd to clay,
> Might stop a hole to keep the wind away.
> O that that earth which kept the world in awe
> Should patch a wall t' expel the winter's flaw!

Elsewhere he says: "A man may fish with the worm
that hath eat of a king, and eat of the fish that hath
fed of that worm . . . a king may go a progress
through the guts of a beggar."

Such talk makes all action and all human endeavor illusory. Why act when this is the fate of us
all? The thought of death is a favorite device for
evading life's demands. Spinoza seems to have
known this when he wrote: "A free person thinks
of nothing less than of death, and his wisdom is oriented toward life."

Thus time passes, and when Hamlet finally de-
cides to proceed with his act of vengeance, it happens with a great number of entanglements, which
claim far more victims than was originally planned.
He himself perishes in the process, and one will do
well not to blame any anonymous fate for it. According to the profound saying of Herodotus with
which Adler prefaced his book *Understanding
Human Nature*, "the destiny of man lies in his soul."
Thus, at the end of Shakespeare's drama, Fortin-
bras, the new ruler of Denmark, can say about Hamlet what might be the epitaph of all neurotics,
though it often is the maxim of their lives as well:

"For he was likely, had he been put on, to have
proved most royal."

Peer Gynt's Neurosis

This third example from world literature can
also be used to demonstrate the individual psychological findings about the laws of human emotional
life. Ibsen's magnificent mystery play, in some respects related to Goethe's *Faust*, lays human nature
bare in a most profound way. To the great Nordic
portrayer of souls, whose plays to a large extent re-
volve about the psychological concept of the *life lie*,
we owe an unparalleled exemplification of the neurotic life-style, for which the dramatist also used unmistakable autobiographical elements. Not only the
music of Grieg but also the meaning and content of
this play have captivated generations of spectators.

At the very beginning of the action Peer Gynt
appears as a dreamer and braggart who seeks to
compensate with dream feats for the low regard
which his environment has for him. His father has
squandered his money and his farm, and the luster
of his childhood has turned into disconsolate poverty, from which Peer escapes into his fantasies,
where he is superior to everyone. When people
mock him, he flings himself to the ground, looks up
at the clouds, and sees himself riding across the sky
as an emperor:

> Down by the road stand the people, a-cluster,
> Doffing their hats, gazing up in a fluster.
> Women are curtsying. Within everyone's ken
> Are Emperor Peer Gynt and his one thousand men.

His dreams of grandeur leave no room for responsibility and fellow feeling. At a wedding he
steals another man's bride, abducts her into the
mountains, and then abandons her, engages in wild

orgies with mountain women, and finally gets into the spectral realm of the trolls and ghosts, where he impregnates the daughter of the mountain king. Since he obviously is a ruthless egotist, he himself is to become a troll and prince in the spectral realm of the trolls and ghosts. The slogan in this subhuman world is "To thyself be enough," and Peer the dreamer has long since made this the maxim by which he wants to arrange his life. And yet he cannot give up human existence; he resists being changed into a troll and puts an end to the spectral spectacle, but he will nevertheless lead his life as a troll in the shape of a human being.

At this crossroads of his life the possibility of a human existence suddenly opens up to him: Solveig, who loves him, could offer him peace and redemption. But Peer Gynt is not yet capable of fellow feeling; his delusions of grandeur and superiority drive him to faraway places, and he flees from a task that would force him to break through the narrow confines of his self. Even the death of his mother, whose pampering evidently fed his unreal dreams of grandeur, does not really shake him up. Afterwards we find him as a wealthy slave trader and exporter of idols, as a prophet with a desert tribe, and finally as an emperor— in an insane asylum in Cairo. Clinging to his striving for godlikeness logically takes him to the delusionary world of the mentally ill, where all those are stranded who cannot escape the deceptions of egocentricity. In this realm Peer can live the childhood dream which he has taken over into his adult life unchanged; as the "emperor of self" he reigns among madmen, who are carrying the antisocial and unrealistic principle of his life *ad absurdum*.

Even when the aging man returns home to Norway, his nature has changed little. Near the coast

he is shipwrecked, and in the face of the saving keel
to which both he and a cook cling he proves to be
the old, unchanged troll who thinks of himself first,
last, and always. In his homeland he is still remem-
bered; people still tell one another his tall tales
about his exploits, but none recognize him or seem
to have kept him in their hearts. In the face of this
situation there takes place the encounter with himself which he has evaded all his life. Now he can
no longer escape the realization that his whole life
has been built on nothing. He peels the layers of an
onion one by one, and this shows him the hollow-
ness and shapelessness of his self, which has never
formed a genuine human relationship. This is what
he says about it:

> The Gyntish self— what can it be
> But wishes, longings, appetites?
> The Gyntish self— it is the sea
> Of exigencies, whims, and rights!
> All that to *my* heart motion's giving;
> All by which I, as I, am living.
> [Translated by R. Ellis Roberts]

In this I he always finds only himself; no other
human being is included in it. This pettiness which
he has disregarded all his life does not come to the
fore until death approaches him. As a small and limited sinner he is not sufficiently evil to go to hell;
he is to be melted down by a button molder like a
button with a manufacturing defect. But his selfhood, whose self-deification has been his only goal
in life, resists this. In the deification of the self he
has lived past his life. Now he is haunted by his
unthought thoughts, the unspoken watchwords, the
unsung songs— in short, everything that he owes
to the world and to his fellowmen. Dewdrops drip-

ping from the branches sing:

> We are unshed tears.
> You never felt it.
> The ice one fears
> We could have melted.
> You've sealed the dart
> Into your heart.
> The wound is mended.
> Our power is ended.

Only one thing could save him from death: proving that he has not completely denied his real self in his selfishness. No matter how concerned they are about the self, egocentricity and selfhood are in truth a pusillanimous and feeble denial of the self; only he has lived in his true self who has risen above it and forgotten it. Peer, who has loved too little, now finds himself in the wasteland of his egocentricity, in his walled-in ego, which threatens to fall prey to death. At that point Solveig, whose love has awaited him over the decades, appears. He has left the happiness at home that he has sought in foreign lands. Thus love is the savior from death and the devil, as is its mission, and man finds the shelter that he vainly sought in riches, power, knowledge, and success in a Thou to whom he turns in love. The sun rises over Peer Gynt after he has been able to cry out, with reference to Solveig's faith, hope, and love:

> My mother, my wife, woman free from all sin,
> O hide me, o hide me therein!

Raskolnikov: Portrait of a Criminal Psyche

Adler regarded Dostoievsky as one of the greatest precursors of his psychology— Dostoievsky, the connoisseur of human nature, who in his profound novels anticipated almost all insights of depth psychology. His descriptions of the human psyche grip us because of the grandiose truths they contain; no psychic condition seems to have been alien to this novelist, in whom Russian literature of the nineteenth century reached its apex. Human existence in all sorts of borderline situations is the real subject of his creativity. The extreme situations which break a person or let him transcend himself constitute the spheres in which Dostoievsky's characters are at home. Their validity and authenticity lie in the fact that they strive, suffer, and go to ruin with unswerving consistency and in accordance with their characters. Such characterizations could have come about only through the profoundest insight into human life, and Nietzsche was right when he wrote these admiring words: "Dostoievsky is the only psychologist from whom I have been able to learn something; he is among the most beautiful strokes of luck in my life."

The novel *Crime and Punishment* confirms Dostoievsky's hardly surpassable psychological intuition. In it the riddle of the criminal psyche is almost completely solved. We may point out that the individual psychological interpretation of delinquency is everywhere in agreement with Dostoievsky's psychology.

According to Adler, we gain a deeper understanding of a delinquent person if we remember that human life has the nature of a task whose accomplishment requires primarily an adequate measure of social interest. Every situation which a person faces puts him to the test of whether or not he has developed sufficient social interest within himself. The more difficult the situation, the more community spirit it requires to be mastered in universally valid fashion and without being deflected to the level of personal superiority, that is, to the egotistic striving for power that tries to disregard reality. To a person who has not been educated to cooperate, crime often appears as a way out, a means of confirming himself. To have the necessary energy for this, the criminal must first surrender to despair; he must silence the voice of social interest in himself so as to be emotionally prepared for his deed. In his aggression against his fellowmen and society he takes revenge for all real and imagined injustices that the world has done him. No matter how miserable and antisocial his deed may be, in his thinking and feeling it becomes an expression of the strength and godlikeness which magically attract all weak and timid minds. The psychological concomitants of crime reveal that it springs from mental illness. In this, too, Dostoievsky was a precursor of depth psychology.

His murderer, Raskolnikov, lies in bed for two months, hungry and feverish, and considers whether he should kill an old woman, a pawnbroker. We learn that he has given up his studies because he no longer has any means of subsistence. He is a proud and lordly person whose sensibilities are hurt by poverty and misery and who compensates for his misfortune in real life with high-flown dreams. With the peculiar logic so characteristic of a diseased psyche he tends toward his crime, which he hopes will solve all his problems. He keeps reminding himself that he will perform a useful function with his deed ("What good is the old usurer?"); he ties his criminal plan to his prestige and his sense of his own value ("Am I Napoleon or am I a louse?"); and finally he convinces himself with conscious and unconscious arguments that his crime is a heroic deed, or at least a necessity.

Dostoievsky gives us precise information about

the way in which the life of his protagonist *telically* leads to the foul deed. Rodion Raskolnikov is a widow's son who was pampered in his youth and approached life with great demands. Life does not offer him the admiration and devotion which his mother and sister bestowed upon him— hence his pride, his reserve, and his implacable attitude toward a reality in which he is in danger of becoming a failure. In his innermost being he revolts against a world which denies him the triumphs that were his without a struggle in childhood.

And yet the road to a criminal act is a long and arduous one. Raskolnikov has to collect a great deal of "tendentious material" before he receives the impetus that propels him over the border of his social interest. The usurious woman takes his last pawn and gives him only a fraction of its value. In a tavern he meets the drunkard Marmeladov, whose dipsomania not only ruins the health of his wife and small children but also turns his oldest daughter Sonia into a prostitute. Raskolnikov's hatred of the human race does not overcome his basically gentle and love-hungry soul, however, until he learns from his mother's letter that his sister wants to marry a rich and unloved man in order to make it possible for him to continue his studies. This fact makes his feeling of inferiority grow to boundless dimensions. Here, too, it is a case of prostitution caused by a good-for-nothing, but this time Raskolnikov takes the place of Marmeladov.

As his pride rears up, his criminal plan assumes ineluctable shape. But there still is unconscious hesitation; it is the voice of fellow feeling in him, which he must silence before he can proceed with his deed. With the aid of a dream he convinces himself that this is the only way he should act.

He dreams of a childhood experience of many years ago. He sees a coachman whose horse, a feeble old mare, has broken down under the load imposed upon her and cannot get up by herself any more. The coachman furiously beats away at the horse, and he is surrounded by a group of curious onlookers who watch this spectacle mockingly and unfeelingly. In this dream scene the voice of the coachman is heard, saying that he is going to beat the mare to death, that she isn't any good any more, she is useless, and it is better to kill her than to let her live. Raskolnikov need not be able to understand and interpret this dream; it is enough for him to derive from it the final impetus, the overcoming of the last inhibitions, unconsciously (though for us the symbolism is evident), for the old mare and the usurer are alike: both are "worthless." Here we recognize the element of devaluation that is never absent in the criminal psyche (perhaps in this vein: "What does one human life matter? There are plenty of people— too many, in fact"). This is a component of an unfeeling view of life born of a pathological will to power.

Long after Raskolnikov has killed the old woman we also learn the theoretical foundations of his deed. Inspector Petrovitch has dug up a periodical article by him in which the "right to crime" is proclaimed. Raskolnikov divides people into common and uncommon ones; the former must live in obedience to the law, while the latter, by virtue of being uncommon, are permitted to break all barriers. These reflections are an apologia for the boundless will to power which pretends to be humane— Raskolnikov asks whether Newton and Kepler would not have had to gain acceptance for their findings even if this had required the price of

human lives— but which at bottom postulates a
false aristocracy of the hard and the unscrupulous.
This *Weltanschauung*, with which the Dostoiev-
skian murderer masks his own cowardice and weakness in the face of life, is the real root of the criminal
psyche, whether it manifests itself within the law
or outside it. Napoleon, whose crimes against humanity were committed under the cloak of legiti-
macy, is reputed to have said: "To a man like me,
a million people are nothing but dirt."

Dostoievsky's poetic understanding of human
nature fills us with the greatest admiration even if
we are not willing to follow his religious and political views. In one of his books Adler impressively
acknowledges his indebtedness to this boldest of all
portrayers of human beings: "Dostoievsky has become a dear and great teacher to us in the most diverse areas . . . His figures, his ethics, and his art
lead us to a profound understanding of human communal life" (*Praxis und Theorie der Individualpsychologie*, pp. 208 ff.).

Bibliography

Works by Alfred Adler

Studie über die Minderwertigkeit von Organen. Vienna, 1907.

Über den nervösen Charakter: Grundzüge einer vergleichenden Individualpsychologie und Psychotherapie. Vienna, 1912 (*The Neurotic Constitution.* New York, 1926).

Die andere Seite: Eine massenpsychologische Studie über die Schuld des Volkes. Vienna, 1919.

Praxis und Theorie der Individualpsychologie: Vorträge zur Einführung in die Psychotherapie für Ärzte, Psychologen und Lehrer. Munich, 1924. (*The Practice and Theory of Individual Psychology.* New York, 1927).

Menschenkenntnis. Leipzig, 1927. (*Understanding Human Nature.* New York, 1927).

Individualpsychologie in der Schule: Vorlesungen für Lehrer und Erzieher. Leipzig, 1929.

Problems of Neurosis: A Book of Case Histories. London, 1929.

The Science of Living. New York, 1929.

The Education of Children. New York, 1930.

The Pattern of Life. New York, 1930.

Das Problem der Homosexualität: Erotisches Training und erotischer Rückzug. Leipzig, 1930.

What Life Should Mean to You. Boston, 1931.

Der Sinn des Lebens. Vienna, 1933. (*Social Interest: A Challenge to Mankind.* New York, 1939).

Religion und Individualpsychologie: Eine prinzipielle Auseinandersetzung über Menschenführung. Vienna, 1933.

Works on Adler and Individual Psychology

Wexberg, Erwin, ed. *Handbuch der Individualpsychologie*. Munich, 1926.

Rühle-Gerstel, Alice. *Der Weg zum Wir*. Dresden, 1927.

Seif, L., and Zilahi, L., eds. *Selbsterziehung des Charakters: Alfred Adler zum 60. Geburtstag gewidmet*. Leipzig, 1930.

Wexberg, Erwin. *Individualpsychologie: Eine systematische Darstellung*. Leipzig, 1931.

Wandeler, J. *Die Individualpsychologie A. Adlers in ihrer Beziehung zur Philosophie des Als Ob H. Vaihingers*. Leipzig, 1932.

Ganz, Madeline. *La psychologie d'Alfred Adler et le développement de l'enfant*. Neuchâtel-Paris, 1935.

Bottome, Phyllis. *Alfred Adler: A Biography*. New York, 1939.

Spiel, Oskar. *Am Schaltbrett der Erziehung*. Vienna, 1947.

Way, Lewis, *Alfred Adler's Place in Psychology*. New York, 1950.

Brachfeld, Oliver. *Minderwertigkeitsgefühle beim Einzelnen und in der Gemeinschaft*. Stuttgart, 1953.

Stern, Erich, ed. *Die Psychotherapie in der Gegenwart*. Zurich, 1958. (Rudolf Dreikurs: "Die Individualpsychologie").

Xylander, Ernst von. *Umgang mit schwierigen Menschen*. Munich-Basel, 1958.

Adler, Kurt A., and Deutsch, Danica, eds. *Essays in Individual Psychology*. New York, 1959.

Ansbacher, Heinz L., and Ansbacher, Rowena R., eds. *The Individual Psychology of Alfred Adler: A Systematic Presentation in Selections from His Writings*. New York, 1959.

Bleidick, Ulrich. *Die Individualpsychologie in ihrer Bedeutung für die Pädagogik*. Mülheim/Ruhr, 1959.

Kausen, Rudolf. *Wege zur Einheit in der Tiefenpsychologie*. Munich-Basel, 1959.

Orgler, Hertha. *Alfred Adler: The Man and His Work*. New York, 1963.

Rattner, Josef. *Psychologie und Psychopathologie des Lie-
    beslebens.* Munich, 1970.
Rattner, Josef. *Alfred Adler in Selbstzeugnissen und Bild-
    dokumenten.* Reinbek bei Hamburg, 1972.
Sperber, Manès. *Masks of Loneliness: Alfred Adler in Per-
    spective.* New York, 1974.

Index